AF568112

FINANCIAL INSTITUTIONS AND ECONOMIC REFORMS

By

Dr. K. Kiran

Teaching Associate
Deptt. of Economics
Dr. B.R. Ambedkar University
Hyderabad
(Andhra Pradesh)

DISCOVERY PUBLISHING HOUSE PVT. LTD.
NEW DELHI-110 002

Published by:
Tilak Wasan

DISCOVERY PUBLISHING HOUSE PVT. LTD.
4831/24, Prahlad Street, Ansari Road
Darya Ganj, New Delhi-110002 (India)
Phone : +91-11-23279245, 43764432
Fax : +91-11-23253475
E-mail : parul.wasan@gmail.com
discoverypublishinghouse@gmail.com
info@discoverypublishinggroup.com
web : www.discoverypublishinggroup.com

First Edition: **2011**
ISBN: 978-81-8356-884-5

Financial Institutions and Economic Reforms

Printed at:
Shree Balaji Art Press
Delhi

Preface

Industrial finance plays a vital role in development of a nation. It accelerates economic growth of a country by enhancing production capacity, creates employment opportunities and it will also be useful to establish balanced regional development. Generally, in developing and underdeveloped economies industries are facing the problem of financial assistance particularly small scale industries. The small scale industries are providing wide range of employment opportunities and bringing substantial amount of foreign reserves. It is with this view special industrial financial institutions were started in India. The services of these institutions are quite impressive for speedy industrial growth. Due to this financial assistance more number of entrepreneurs obtaining assistance in general, first generation entrepreneurs in particular. In the globalization scenario competition among the nations is unavoidable and inescapable. To face this competition institutional finance is inevitable.

To meet this objective Andhra Pradesh Government has set up an institution namely Andhra Pradesh State Financial Corporation, APSFC, in 1956 with the principal objective of creating finance to small and medium entrepreneurs throughout the state there by assisting in establishment, promotion, improvement and development of industries. The present study examines tremendous changes that are occurred during pre and post reform period. The book highlights the growth of financial assistance in respect of its size, changes in its organizational structure and the occurrence of diversification and innovations and practices.

The time span covered in the book is a fairly long one. The detailed discussion covers the study period starting from 1975-76 to 2005-06. But in order to observe and to place this discussion the changes that took place during reform period, the entire study period is divided into two sub periods by taking 1990-91 as bench mark period. The period 1975-76 to 1990-91 is chosen as pre-reform period and 1991-92 to 2005-06 taken as post-reform period.

The study is organized into six chapters. Chapter-I presents the introduction, evolution of SFCs in India, need for the study and objectives of the study along with the methodology. Chapter-II deals with the profile of APSFC along with the SFC Act. The role of APSFC in achieving balanced regional development, through extending assistance to backward regions and backward districts is analyzed in chapter III. The APSFC's assistance to SSIs, MSIs units is presented in Chapter-IV. The performance of APSFC in terms of sanctions, disbursements, recoveries and profits are examined in chapter V. The role of APSFC in the generation of employment and in extending assistance to first generation entrepreneurs belonging to weaker sections, with a specific focus on their financial inclusion. Summary, conclusions and policy prescriptions are given in chapter-VI.

This research work was under taken for the award of Ph. D degree in Andhra University during 2005-09 under the guidance of Prof. K. Siva Prasad. I am deeply indebted to him for his constant encouragement and constructive criticism throughout the study. I have also benefited greatly from the discussions I had with my joint director Prof. K. Sree Rama Murty. My thanks are also due to Mr. A. Vamsi Krushna and Mr. D. Venkata Rao, for shaping the thesis in a neat form. In preparation of the study, at various stages, I received encouragement and invaluable help in some form or other from my friends and well wishers who are too numerous to be mentioned here. To all of them I am grateful. I am also indebted to Discovery Publishing House Pvt. Ltd., Delhi for publishing this book.

I express my heartfelt thanks to the Almighty for his continuous blessings.

DR. K. KIRAN

Contents

—Assistance to Hospitals/Nursing Homes—Assistance for Acquiring Electro Medical Equipment—Assistance for Setting up of Industrial Estates—Single Window Scheme—Road Laying work under build operate Transport Scheme—Scheme for Qualified Professionals—Mahila Udyam Nidhi Scheme—National Equity Fund Scheme—Super Entrepreneur's Scheme—General Entrepreneur++ Scheme (GES ++)—General Entrepreneurs Scheme A+ (GES A+)—Senior Successful Entrepreneur Scheme—Scheme for Acquisition of ISC 9000 Series Certificates by SSI Units—Marketing Assistance Scheme for SSI Products—Working Capital Term Loan—Self-employment for the Ex-servicemen—Term Loan to Practicing Doctors—Credit Linked Capital Subsidy Scheme for Technology Upgradation of SSI Units—Super Bazar or Retail out lets Scheme for Marketing of SSI Products and others—Scheme for Export-oriented Units—Working Capital Term Loan for Seasonal Industries—Scheme for Establishment, Expansion and Moderni-zation/Technology Upgradation of food processing industries and other Related Industries—Scheme for financial assistance for setting up private market yards—Scheme for Financial Assistance to Sc/St Entre-preneurs for Setting up of Industrial Units and Service Enterprises—Scheme for financial assistance to women entre-preneurs for setting up of industrial units and service enterprises—Scheme-wise Classification of Sanctions Made by APSFC During 1990-91 to 2005-06—Scheme-wise Classification of Disbursements made by APSF During 1990-91 to 2005-06—Number of Sanctions Assisted by the Corporation to weaker Sections During 1991-92 to 2005-06—Amount of Sanctions made by the Corporation to Weaker Sections—Number of Disbursements made by the Corporation to Weaker Sections During 1991-92 to 2005-06—Amount of Disbursements made by the Corporation to Weaker Sections During 1991-92 to 2005-06—Number of

CHAPTER

Introduction

Origin of Financial Institutions

The economic development of any country depends on the extent to which its financial system efficiently and effectively mobilizes and allocates its resources. Though there are a number of banks and financial institutions in the country, some financial institutions are assigned to perform special task of fostering the development of the nation. These institutions not only provide medium- and long-term financial assistance but also act as catalytic agents in promoting balanced development of the country. These are engaged in promotion and development of industry, agriculture and other key sectors. They also provide development services that are essential in accelerating growth of an economy.

Financial sector plays an indispensable role in the overall development of a country. The most important constituent of this sector is the financial institutions, which act as a conduit for the transfer of resources from net savers to net borrowers. The financial institutions have traditionally been the major source of long-term funds for the economy. These institutions provide a variety of financial products and services to fulfil the varied needs of the commercial sector. Besides, they provide assistance to new enterprises, small and medium firms as well as to the industries, that are established in backward areas. Thus, they have helped in reducing regional disparities by inducing widespread industrial development.

The need for development of financial institutions was felt very strongly, the moment India attained Independence. The country needed a strong capital goods sector to support and accelerate the pace of industrialization. The existing industries required long-term funds for their reconstruction, modernization, expansion and diversification programmes, while the new industries required enormous investments for setting up of gigantic projects in the capital sector. However, there were gaps in banking system and capital markets which needed to be filled to meet this enormous requirement of funds. In order to fill these gaps, new institutional machinery was devised with the setting up of special financial institutions which would provide the necessary financial resources and know-how, so as to foster the industrial growth in the country.

In India the first step was taken towards building up a structure of development financial institutions in 1948, by establishing the Industrial Finance Corporation of India (IFCI). This institution was set up with an Act of Parliament with a view to provide medium and long-term credit to units in the corporate sector and industrial concerns.

In view of the immensity of the task and vast size of the country it was not possible for a single institution to cater to the financial needs of small industries spread across different States. Hence, the necessity for setting up financial institutions across the country to cater to the needs of small and medium scale industries was recognized. Accordingly, the State Financial Corporation Act was passed in 1951 to establish State Financial Corporations (SFCs) in different States of India.

At present the country is being served by 57 financial institutions, comprising 11 institutions at the national level and 46 institutions at the State level. These financial institutions have a wide network of branches and are supported by technical consultancy organisations with Industrial Development Bank of India (IDBI) acting as the apex institution for coordinating them and to devise financing and promotional activities. Their strategies, policies and industrial promotional efforts sub serve the national objectives of rapid industrialization growth, balanced regional development, creation of new class of entrepreneurs, and providing self employment opportunities.

The financial institutions were financing in a highly regulated regime up to 1991. In the wake of globalization and liberalization, the financing requirements of the corporate sector have undergone a tremendous change. Many foreign players entered into strategic alliance with Indian firms. There was an increase in research and development activities as well as the diversification plans of firms. Investment in technology and infrastructure became crucial.

The Government of India, in order to provide adequate supply of credit to various sectors of the economy, has evolved a well developed structure of financial institutions in the country. These financial institutions can be broadly categorized into All-India Institutions and State Level Institutions, depending upon the geographical coverage of their operations. At the national level, they provide long- and medium-term loans at reasonable rates of interest. They subscribe to the debentures issues by the companies, underwrite public issue of shares, guarantee loans and deferred payments, etc. Though, the State Level Institutions are mainly concerned with the development of medium and small scale enterprises, they provide the same type of financial assistance as that of the national level institutions.

In this context, the state financial corporation has been playing a vital role to strengthening of Small Scale Industries (SSIs) and Medium Scale Industries (MSIs). State Financial Corporations (SFCs) are the State level financial institutions which play a crucial role in the development of small and medium enterprises in the concerned States. They provide financial assistance in the form of term loans, direct subscription to equity/debentures, guarantees, discounting of bills of exchange and seed/special capital, etc. The SFCs have been set up with the objective of facilitating higher investments, generating greater employment and widening the ownership base of industries. The SFCs have also started providing assistance to newer types of business activities such as floriculture, tissue culture, poultry farming, commercial complexes and services related to engineering, marketing, etc. There are 18 State Financial Corporations (SFCs) in the country of which 17 were setup under the SFC Act, 1951. The Tamil Nadu Industrial Investment Corporation Limited established in 1949 under the Companies Act.

An entrepreneur requires a continuous flow of funds not only for setting up of his/her business, but also for successful operation as well as regular up gradation/modernization of the industrial unit. To meet this requirement, the Government (both at the Central and State level) has been undertaking several steps like setting up of banks and financial institutions; formulating various policies and schemes, etc. All such measures are specifically focused towards the promotion and development of small and medium enterprises. In view of the changing business environment, SFCs are focusing more attention on investment activities and corporation related operations. With ongoing liberalization in the country, the SFCs have to play a more challenging role than earlier.

In the light of this background, the Andhra Pradesh State Financial Corporation (APSFC) was established in 1956, for promoting small- and medium-scale industries in Andhra Pradesh under the provisions of the Sate Financial Corporations Act, 1951. The Corporation came into existence on 1st November, 1956 by merger of Andhra State Financial Corporation and Hyderabad State Financial Corporation. The Corporation has launched many entrepreneur-friendly schemes to provide term loans, working capital term loans, special and seed capital assistance to suit the needs of various categories of entrepreneurs. The Corporation has completed five decades of dedicated service in industrial financing of tiny, small and medium scale sector units and contributing to the balanced regional development of the State.

The APSFC has been a part and parcel of industrial growth of Andhra Pradesh for over five decades in the service of small and medium scale sectors focusing on industrial finance areas. Though many of the SFCs in the country found it difficult to continue their reforms, the APSFC withstood the transition process with confidence and with re-oriented corporate culture, work ethics and value systems. APSFC is also an ISO 9001-2000 Organisation for all its simplified and streamlined processes and adherence to quality standards in processes. It built up internal competence creating customer friendly systems.

The corporation is an entrepreneur-friendly organisation with strong bonds and lasting relations to provide all financial facilities under one roof. The APSFC has been making MOUs with Commercial Banks for arranging working capital loans. In short, it is a friendly financier of the State industries.

It has also set for itself ambitious targets in the key operational areas and keeping in view, the priorities laid down in the State Government's Industrial Investment 2010, APSFC has been dedicating and motivating its work force for strengthening the financial services to industries.

Need for the Study

Financial adequacy is one of the important problems of Small-Scale and Medium Scale Industries. To improve the financial position of these units, some of the financial institutions such as Industrial Development Bank of India, Andhra Pradesh Industrial Development Corporation, Andhra Pradesh State Financial Corporation and other Commercial Banks have been financing the small and medium scale industries. Of these financial institutions, Andhra Pradesh State Financial Corporation stands as one of the major financial contributor to this sector. Hence, the study is centralized on this

Corporation. In Andhra Pradesh there are a number of research studies focusing on the APSFC assistance to SSIs and MSIs. However, the studies comparing the performance of APSFC during pre- and post-reform periods are very few. As such, the present study is attempted in this direction.

Objectives of the Study

The present study aims at making a comparative assessment of the performance of the APSFC during pre- and post-reform periods. More specifically, the objectives are as follows:

1. To examine the role of APSFC in promoting balanced regional development.
2. To analyse the industry-wise assistance made by APSFC.
3. To evaluate the performance of APSFC in the areas of sanctions, disbursements and recoveries.
4. To find out the role of APSFC as catalyst for generation of employment.
5. To study APSFC's assistance to weaker sections of the society so as to examine their financial inclusion.
6. To suggest measures for improving the performance of the APSFC.

Methodology

In order to examine the role of APSFC during the pre- and post-reform periods, the year 1991 is taken as a bench mark to arrive at the pre-reform period and post-reform period. Besides taking 1991 as the dividing line for the pre- and post-reform periods, a 15-year period ending with 1991, i.e. 1976-77 to 1990-91 is chosen as the pre-reform period and a 15-year period spreading over 1991-92 to 2005-06 is taken to represent the post-reform period.

The APSFC being regional development bank supposed to under taken not merely term lending operations but also in relation to promotional activities also. Due to resource constraints the emphasis still continued to be on term lending operations only. Hence, its operational performance is studied more on the basis of data pertaining to sanctions and disbursements. The study tries to examine the hypotheses that the performance of APSFC during the post-reform period is impressive in terms of assistance to priority sectors and in terms of loan recoveries. It is also proposed to test the hypothesis that the performance of APSFC in terms of financial inclusion of weaker sections, i.e SCs, STs, minorities is better when compared to other caste groups.

Tools of Analysis

Various statistical tools such as percentages, averages, and correlations are used to process the data. Simple growth rates, exponential and liner growth rates are calculated to examine and analyse the trends and patterns in the growth of assistance deployed by APSFC. It is proposed to study the diversification of sanctions and disbursements at beginning and end of the both reform periods using Herfindahl Index.

Simple Growth Rates

It gives the percentage increase over the previous year, i.e.

$$g = \left(\frac{y_t - y_{t-1}}{y_{t-1}} \right) 100$$

Where 'g' is the growth rate and y_t and y_{t-1} are the values of variable y in year t-1 respectively.

Exponential Growth Rate

It works out change for a given period on the basis of the base year and end years' value.

$$y = a\, e^{bt}$$

$$\log y_e = \log a.\, b^t$$

where,

$$b = \frac{\Delta y / y}{\Delta t}$$

Karl Pearson's Co-efficient of Correlation (R)

Correlation (r) is calculated to examine the extent or degree of correlation between two variables. The association between the following variables is examined: (*a*) between the number of applications dealt and the number of applications sanctioned, (*b*) sanctions and disbursements and (*c*) disbursements and recoveries.

$$\text{Correlation (r)} : \frac{\frac{1}{n_i = 1} n \, \varepsilon x \, iyi - \bar{x}_1 \bar{y}}{Sx \quad Sy}$$

Where x_i = Observation on variable x, i=1, 2, . . . n

y_i = Observation on variables y, i= 1, 2, . . . n

$\bar{x}$ = A.M. of x and S_x = S.D of x

$\bar{y}$ = A.M. of y and S_y = S.D. of y

$$r = \frac{\varepsilon dxdy}{\sqrt{\varepsilon dx^2 \; \varepsilon dy^2}}$$

Herfindahl Index Number

As APSFC chanallizes its assistance to different regions in Andhra Pradesh, it is thought fit to study the diversification of sanctions and disbursements at the beginning and end of the both the periods using Herfindahl Index. The Herfindahl index can be written as follows.

$$H = \sum_{i=1}^{n} x_i^2 \div (n_{\varepsilon} xi)^2$$

i = 1 . . . N regions identified.

x_i = The amount of assistance to each region i and Σx is the total assistance.

Regression

Regression analysis is used to identify the recovery factors affecting the disbursements made by APSFC. In this connection two explanatory variables, namely Principal Recovery and

Interest Amount Collected by APSFC are taken. The impact of these two variables is estimated through two variable analysis. In this connection both linear and log linear {Cobb Doglous} functional forms are used in the estimation.

Data Sources

The study is based on the secondary data. The data pertaining to this study period (1976-77 to 2005-06) are collected from Annual Reports of Andhra Pradesh State Financial Corporation (APSFC), Annual Reports of Industrial Development Bank of India (IDBI), Reserve Bank of India (RBI), Annual Reports, Small Industries Development Bank of India (SIDBI), Annual Statistical Abstracts and Hand Books published by the Directorate of Planning and Statistics of Andhra Pradesh, and other related issues and journals.

Design of the Study

The study is organized into seveen chapters. Chapter 1 presents the introduction, evolution of SFCs in India, need for the study and the objectives of the study along with the methodology. Chapter 2 deals with the profile of APSFC along with the SFC Act. The role of APSFC in achieving balanced regional development, through extending assistance to backward regions and backward districts is analyzed in Chapter 3. The APSFC's assistance to SSIs, MSIs units is presented in Chapter 4. The performance of APSFC in terms of sanctions, disbursements, recoveries and profits are examined in Chapter 5. The role of APSFC in the generation of employment and in extending assistance to first generation entrepreneurs belonging to weaker sections, with a specific focus on their financial inclusion and summary, conclusions and policy prescriptions are analyzed in Chapter-6.

Limitations of the Study

The present study has some limitations. The total expenditure of APSFC which is spent on administrative costs and borrowing costs could not be analyzed due to data constraints. The performance of units assisted by APSFC are not covered in the study. Further, the analysis pertaining to assistance extended to first generation entrepreneurs through different schemes relating to employment generation, value of output is confined only to fifteen years i.e. 1991-92 to 2005-06, due to non-availability of data.

CHAPTER

2

A Profile of the Andhra Pradesh State Financial Corporation

Origin of APSFC

With the dawn of Independence, India set before itself the objective of fostering entrepreneurship and creation of employment through the promotion and development of large and small scale industries. In order to develop the necessary industrial base, adequate credit support measures were also initiated in the country. In this chapter an attempt is made to present the profile of the Andhra Pradesh State Financial Corporation. The Industrial Finance Corporation of India (IFCI) was set up in 1948 to provide financial assistance to large industry. The State Financial Corporations Act, 1951 paved the way for establishment of State Financial Corporations to support Small and Medium Scale Industries (SMIs) in the respective States. Andhra Pradesh State was formed on 1st November, 1956. On the same day, the Andhra Pradesh State Financial Corporation (APSFC) came into existence with the amalgamation of the erstwhile Andhra State Financial Corporation and Hyderabad State Financial Corporation with the mandate to promote and develop small and medium industries in the State of Andhra Pradesh. As such 1st November, 1956 is a golden letter day for Andhra Pradesh State.

Capital Structure

The APSFC started with paid-up equity capital of Rs. 1.50 crores in 1956 which now stands at Rs. 92.22 crores against an authorized capital of Rs. 500 crores. The Government of Andhra Pradesh holds 68.40 per cent and IDBI 31.31 per cent equity while, the remaining share of 0.29 per cent is held by LIC and individual shareholders.

A Galaxy of Distinguished Chairmen

The First Chairman was Sri Bikkani Venkataratnam, a respected co-operator, who guided the Corporation for eleven years. He was succeeded by Sri Maddi Sudharshanam, an industrialist who was at the helm for eight years and Sri KLN Prasad, an industrialist and later on, Member of Parliament. He was followed by a succession of able Chairman.

Reach and Outreach

The Corporation with its head office at Hyderabad in 1956 had only one branch at Vijayawada. During 1972-73, the Corporation opened two more branches at Visakhapatnam and Tirupati. In 1975-76, the Corporation opened six one-man offices in six districts. Now it has a network of 25 branches covering all the 23 districts of Andhra Pradesh and one extra branch each in Rangareddy and Medak Districts. It new Head Office building i.e., North Block was constructed during 1976 and South Block constructed during 1978 in Chirag Ali Lane, Hyderabad. The location and scope for further expansion will enable the Corporation to undertake new activities for the development of Small and Medium Enterprises (SME) Sector. The Corporation introduced computerization in 1980-81 which initiative has paid good returns. Today, all the Branches are computerized and connected through dedicated 64 Kpbs lines. Customized software seamlessly provides good service.

Impressive Term Loans

The APSFC generally gives term loan assistance up to Rs. 2 crores for sole proprietary and partnership firms, up to Rs. 5

crores to companies and co-operative societies. Small Scale Industrial Development Bank of India (SIDBI) has permitted the Corporation to extend loans up to Rs. 20 crores under special circumstances.

An Engine of Growth

In the first year of its operations (1956), APSFC sanctioned Rs. 91.15 lakhs to 51 units and disbursed Rs. 33 lakhs with focus on tiny and small scale units and employment-oriented SSI units. By the end of 1976, the sanctions rose to Rs. 60.89 crores covering 4,079 units. By the year 1988-89, the cumulative sanctions reached Rs. 1000 crore mark, benefiting 38,389 industrial and service enterprises. The cumulative sanctions crossed Rs. 5,500 crores mark in 2004-05 with the number of assisted units crossing 85,000. By assisting in the capital formation of over Rs. 12,000 crores and generating employment for 8.50 lakh persons, the Corporation created a golden record in the State. During the year 2005-06, while the sanctions stood at Rs. 58,596.93 lakhs, the disbursements accounted for Rs. 42,172.45 lakhs. The Corporation has given priority to the sectors of the state economy which have good growth prospects, competitive advantage and can create employment and beneficial multiplier effect.

A Role Model and Lead State Financial Corporation

In 1978-79, the Corporation switched over from the Mercantile Accounting System to Cash System. It built up internal competence through training of employees, streamlining systems and effective implementation of Government Programmes. In 1979-80, the Corporation became the lead State Financial Corporation in the country with the highest sanctions, disbursements and recoveries. It maintained its lead position in 1980-81 also with sanctions exceeding Rs. 47 crores.

Balanced Regional Development

The Corporation also seeks to play the role of a facilitator and catalyst in encouraging entrepreneurship and securing balanced regional development. As such, the highest number of sanctions was made to the Telangana region, which was considered to be a backward region in the State of Andhra Pradesh. In 1976, the units set up in Telangana accounted for 47 per cent of the total sanctioned amount. This figure rose to 55 per cent during 1986 and by the year 2000 it was 57 per cent. Up to 2005 this trend continued.

Provisioning Norms and Transitional Woes

In the wake of economic reforms, provisioning norms were introduced with effect from 1993-94. The Corporation was required to provide Rs. 105.22 crores towards provisioning as on 31st March, 1994. Though, APSFC was continuously earning operating profits the net-profits slipped into the red. It took time for the Corporation to recover from the setback as the State Government in the meantime had stopped equity support amidst the talk of privatization and closure of public sector enterprises.

Attuning to the Times for a Turn-Around

The 21st century cannot be tackled with the technology, tools and techniques of the 20th century. The Corporation attuned itself to the 2K mode and made a *de novo* attempt to effectively turn around the Corporation with a series of well-coordinated steps with sharp focus, team-work, networking and better customer relationships. The professional background of the employees, coupled with their knowledge of industries and entrepreneurship and their determined efforts ensured the success of the turnaround.

Vision, Mission and Passion Converge

With the amendments of SFCs Act in 2000, SIDBI appointed Sri M Gopalakrishna, IAS (Retd.) as non-executive Chairman in February 2002. With the support of the Government of Andhra Pradesh and SIDBI, the Board was reconstituted. A revised strategy comprising good governance policies and best practices was put into effect. The Corporation was able to galvanize and harmonize the dynamic leadership of the Managing Directors with the enthusiastic and dedicated efforts of the employees to bring about a remarkable turn-around.

A Tradition of Operating Profits

The Corporation was a continuously profit-making public sector organization for 37 years from 1956-57 to 1992-93 which is a creditable record indeed. The profit of Rs. 4.32 lakhs in the maiden year 1956-57 went up to Rs. 102.24 lakhs in 1976-77 and to Rs. 546.90 lakhs by the end of 1985-86. Consequent upon the introduction of provisioning norms, the Corporation could not make profits between 1993-94 and 2001-02. However, the Corporation slowly gained momentum and posted a net profit of Rs. 783.63 lakhs by 2005-06.

the Scenario Changes—Profits Increase

The Corporation recorded a net profit of Rs. 2.36 crores in the year 2002-03 after a long lapse of nine years. Prepayments of high cost loans was done and recoveries improved. Subsequently, the Non-Performing Assets were also reduced. Sanctions and disbursements registered an impressive increase. In the next year, profit increased to Rs. 10.10 crores, and in the following year (2004-05), profits reached a record of Rs. 13.15 crores. Its turnaround was remarkable despite the fact that there was no capital infusion except for an equity contribution of Rs. 2.00 crores from the State Government during the year 2003-04 and Rs. 2.50 crores during the year 2004-05.

APSFC—The 'Numero UNO'—The Mark of Pure Gold

APSFC became the lead SFC among the 18 SFCs in the country in 2001-02 in respect of sanctions, disbursements and recovery percentage. It has since maintained the position for four years in a row with increased net profits. The Corporation has learnt the secret of doing homework, putting in hard work, smart work, teamwork and above all the required network.

Eligible and Creditable Institution

The APSFC now has an enviable record of five decades of prompt repayment of all its loans to its lenders and a solid reputation for credit-worthiness and professional management. This has prompted the Small Industries Development Bank of India (SIDBI) to enter into a Memorandum of Understanding (MoU) with the Corporation and offer refinance at lower rates of interest to assist Small Scale industries. It has also made APSFC an eligible institution to draw amounts from the Small and Medium Enterprises Fund. The Government of Andhra Pradesh has also declared the Corporation as an eligible institution for accepting deposits under its fixed deposits scheme from Government Departments, Quasi-government Bodies and Public Sector Undertakings. The Corporation has been receiving enthusiastic support from all its depositors.

Longevity, the Hallmark of Service to Society

The APSFC has completed more than of 50 years of dedicated service and has the satisfaction of having served well and built a durable and resilient organization with a strong corporate culture, work ethic and value system. Its longevity relevance and service is a result of pervasive professionalism, good customer relationship, sense of Corporate Social Responsibility and adoption of the best tenets of Corporate Governance.

Part of Life and Industry in Andhra Pradesh

The APSFC has been a part of life and Industry in Andhra Pradesh for three generations. It is visualizing an even a greater role and as such keen to play a larger part in industrial development as partner in progress and prosperity. The APSFC renews its pledge of selfless service to the Small and Medium Industries to secure a golden future for industrial and economic growth and usher in prosperity.

Entrepreneurship

The APSFC has been playing a dynamic role in encouraging entrepreneurship, perceiving opportunities and helping entrepreneurs. Playing the role of a Coach, Mentor and Catalyst with consummate ease and grace, it has guided many First Generation Entrepreneurs to achieve success. The APSFC believes that "when preparation meets opportunity, success follows". That is the key to fostering good entrepreneurship. The APSFC had an uncanny knack of picking up and honouring entrepreneurs with promise by giving *"Parishramika Vijetha Awards"*. The APSFC swells with pride when its entrepreneurs, who start small, grow fast and become big and emerge as global players.

Customer Relationships

To maintain long term customer relationships, it has categorised its customers as 'Good', 'Senior Successful' and 'Super Entrepreneurs', based on their track record and is offering special concessions. As a result of its thoughtful and customer-oriented schemes, APSFC has become the truly investor-friendly financier. The feedback of our customers has been our feed-forward in policy formulation and implementation. It is an article of faith with APSFC that it should "not merely lend, but comprehend and tend" the customer and the industry. This has been the secret of its success. It has been conducting "One Day Entrepreneurs Awareness Seminars" (ODEAS) in all important towns in the State to mobilize and advise entrepreneurs on the prospects for industry in different districts and in rural areas since 1998. The ODEAS programme is now being emulated by other SFCs and Banks in other states of India. This pioneering role continues in all its activities and has resulted in focused customer orientation. Its 'forte' has been the development of entrepreneurship in Andhra Pradesh, which has now become the prime mover of economic growth and definer of a golden future.

Citizen's Charter

APSFC issued a Citizen's Charter in prescribing time limits for clearance of applications and for redressing grievances, anticipating the needs of its clients as now envisaged in the

Right to Information Act. Regular feed-back received from the customers indicates growing confidence in the ability to deliver and making APSFC the cynosure of other SFCs.

The Holy Grail—Commitment to Quality Standards

The APSFC was the first SFC and the first State Public Sector Enterprise to secure ISO 9002-1994 in the year 2001, which was soon upgraded in the year 2002 to ISO 9001-2000 for all its activities and offices indicating its commitment and adherence to standards in products and processes. Thus, it has become the standard-bearer and path-setter for promotion of the quality movement among small and medium industries in Andhra Pradesh. It also provides interest concession for ISO certified clients.

Knowledge—The Driver of Growth

The APSFC believes that creation of knowledge must lead to its fast dissemination and more importantly, its faster application. All its records and accounts are computerized leading to faster sanctions, disbursements and recoveries. A massive programme of training has made its staff not only computer literate but computer savvy. The APSFC has gladly shared its experience and encouraged sister SFCs in the matter of standardization of systems, methods and good practices. It provided a special computer package for financial services and accounting to the Afro-Asian Games held in Hyderabad in 2003 which was widely appreciated as an example of professionalism and corporate social responsibility. The APSFC believes in long-term customer-relationship, which is reflected in the retentiveness of customers, many of whom are repeat customers for the Corporation.

One Stop Finance Shop

To provide all financial facilities under one roof, APSFC has become a "One Stop Finance Shop" and sells insurance products and Government of India Relief Bonds. The

Corporation also secured Corporate Agency for Insurance from IFFCO-TOKIO General Insurance Company to grow a new line of business.

Looking Beyond—Set and Ready to Go

Though APSFC has learned to survive, to strive and to thrive, it has to traverse many a mile more. It is gearing itself to meet the needs, expectations, aspirations and global ambitions of its entrepreneurs and to keep pace with and be ahead of the Industrial Investment Promotion Policy (2005-2010) of the State Government.

A Proud Record of APSFC—The Silver Jubilee Year and Heralds It's Golden Jubilee Year

In 1980-81, Sri. R. Surender Reddy was the Chairman when the Corporation celebrated its Silver Jubilee Year with sanctions of Rs. 47.38 crores and disbursements of Rs. 30.65 crores. The sanctions crossed Rs. 200.00 crores for the first time while disbursements crossed Rs. 100 crores creating a new land mark. The Corporation has become a force to be reckoned with by assisting 17,223 units with a cumulative sanction of Rs. 217.00 crores.

SFC Act

The State Financial Corporation Act is specially incorporated to strengthen State financial corporations in India to assist the small and medium scale units. All state financial corporations have been function according to this Act. The Act has been amended from time to time to suit the requirements of SSIs and MSIs. With this Act, the state financial corporations have been expanding their unprecedented operations to small and medium scale industries in respective states. The Act also states the procedures for appointing of Board of Directors, voting process of the share holders, payment of amounts etc. Some of the salient features of the SFC Act have been presented below:

Management

The general superintendence, direction and management of the affairs and business of the Financial Corporation shall vest in a Board of Directors, which may exercise all powers and do all such acts and things, as may be exercised or done by the Financial Corporation. The Board may direct that any power exercisable by it under this Act shall also be exercisable in such cases and subject to such conditions, if any, as may be specified by it, by the chairman, managing director or the whole-time director.

Board of Directors

The Board of directors shall consist of the following, namely:

(I) A Director to be nominated as Chairman and (II) Two Directors nominated by the State Government of whom one director shall be a person who has special knowledge of or experience in small-scale industries:

The Act provides that in the case of a Joint Financial Corporation, the number of directors shall be such as the State Governments of the participating States may, by agreement among themselves, think fit to nominate each participating State Government, nominating not more than two directors. Further, that in the case of a Joint Financial Corporation, the director, who shall have special knowledge of, or experience in small-scale industries, shall be nominated by that participating State, which according to the terms of agreement between the participating States is entitled to make such nomination.

Term Office of Directors

A nominated director shall hold office during the pleasure of the authority nominating him. The nominated director shall hold office for such term not exceeding three years and shall also be eligible for re-nomination, the Act states that no such Director shall hold office continuously for a period exceeding six years.

An elected Director other than a Director deemed to be elected shall hold office for three years and shall also be eligible for re-election. No such Director shall hold office continuously for a period exceeding six years.

Disqualifications for being a Director

No person shall be a director, if he has been found to be of unsound mind by a court of competent jurisdiction and the finding is in force; or at any time has been, adjudicated as insolvent or has suspended payment of his debts or has compounded with his creditors.

Removal of Director from Office

The State Government may remove from office any Director who is, or has become, subject to any of the disqualifications mentioned in section 12 of the Act.

Chairman of Board

The Small Industries Bank shall, in consultation with the State Government nominate a Director as a Chairman of the Board for such period not exceeding three years and on such terms and conditions as the Small Industries Bank may specify the Chairman shall not be a whole-time Director, unless he is also appointed to function as the Managing Director. He shall preside over the meetings of the Board and the general meetings of the Financial Corporation.

Remuneration of Directors

The Directors other than the Managing Director and not being servants of the Government shall be paid such fees as may be prescribed for attending meetings of the Board. The Director received such salary and allowances and be subject to other terms and conditions of service as the Board may, with the previous approval of the State Government, determine.

Executive Committee

The Board constitutes an Executive Committee consisting of the Chairman and Managing Director, the whole-time directors and such other directors. The Executive Committee shall discharge such functions as may be prescribed or as may be delegated to it by the Board. The Board may constitute such other committees whether consisting wholly of directors or wholly of other persons or partly of directors and partly of other persons for such purpose or purposes as it may think fit.

Meetings of the Board and Committee

The Board and the Executive Committee shall meet at such times and places and shall observe such rules of procedure in regard to transaction of business at its meetings as may be provided by regulations made under this Act. All questions at a meeting shall be decided by a majority of votes of the members present, and, in the case of equality of votes, the Chairman or in his absence, any other person presiding shall have a second or casting vote.

Powers of Executive Committee

Subject to such general or special directions as the Board may from time to time give, the Executive Committee may deal with any matter within the competence of the Board. The minutes of every meeting of the Executive Committee shall, after confirmation thereof at the next meeting of the Executive Committee, be laid before the Board at the next following meeting of the Board.

Advisory Committee

The State Financial Corporation may appoint one or more committee or committees consisting wholly of Directors or wholly of other persons or partly of Directors and partly of other persons for the purpose of assisting the Financial Corporation in the efficient discharge of its functions and, in particular, for the purpose of securing that those functions are exercised with due regard to the circumstances and conditions prevailing in, and the requirements of, particular areas or industries.

Officers and other Employees of the Financial Corporation

The Financial Corporation may appoint such officers, advisers and employees as it considers necessary for the efficient performance of its functions, and determine, by regulations, their conditions of appointment and service and the remuneration payable to them.

Offices and Agencies

The Financial Corporation can establish its head office and other offices and agencies at such places as the State Government may, from time to time, specify and save as aforesaid, the Financial Corporation may establish additional offices or agencies in such other places within the State as it may consider necessary.

The account given above throws light on the structure of APSFC. In the light of this background, at attempt is made in the following chapters to examine the role of APSFC in the industrial development of the State of Andhra Pradesh.

REFERENCES

1. Various Annual Reports and other Reports of APSFC.
2. SFC Act 2000.

CHAPTER

3

The Role of APSFC in Balanced Regional Development

Introduction

Regional imbalances are found in most of the countries of the world. There may be only difference in the degree of imbalances in the developed countries. The problems in these countries are confined only to a few areas and these areas are found to be lagging behind in the process of development relatively to the most developed. But in developing countries these problems often assume serious proportions. The size and nature of the problems in these countries are different in the sense that there are only a few highly developed areas in the midst of large portions of the country which are underdeveloped.

Empirical studies in economic growth in different countries indicate that development does not take place everywhere at the same time. When the process starts, some areas are favored while others are neglected. To quote Friedman and Alonso: ". . . during the period of early industrialization when, for variety of reasons, activities come to be concentrated in one or few centres. These centres not only grow so rapidly as to create problems of entirely new dynamic elements from also more static regions. The remainder of the country is thus relegated to a second class, peripheral postion"[1]

In this context, an attempt has been made in the first section to throw light on the need for balanced regional development. In the second section region-wise sanctions and disbursements during the pre and post reform periods are analyzed. In the third section trends pertaining to sanctioned loans during the pre and post reform period are examined. The fourth section deals with Andhra Pradesh State Financial Corporation (APSFC) branch expansion in each district along with the sanctioned amounts.

SECTION I
NEED FOR BALANCED REGIONAL DEVELOPMENT

The need for reducing imbalances can be argued from different angles. Correcting regional imbalance is crucial from the point of accelerating the growth of the economy. Complementary relationship between reduction in regional disparities and accelerated economic growth is evident. It has been increasingly realised that the national income of a country can be increased tremendously not only by proper utilization, and exploitation of resources available but also diverting them in a planned manner to the relatively depressed areas. It is also clear that the resources at the local level are highly elastic and that they can be used by proper method of regional planning.

It is believed that income inequalities can be reduced by way of reducing regional imbalances. Social justice demands that all citizens are to be treated alike and given an equal opportunity in life. This can be made possible only when inter-regional disparities in the levels of development are bridged and narrowed down. Hence, the idea of balanced regional development has been mooted as a corrective measure in the process of economic development. If this is neglected and unchecked, several regional disputes may occur and may result in numerous economic and social problems.

The reasons for the existence of regional imbalances may be attributed, in addition to several others, to natural resource endowment, differences in productivity growth rates, availability of capital and skilled labour. However, the fact remains that the extent of inequality during the early stages of economic development of a country would be greater than it is in the later and advanced stage of development. It may be said that as the economy moves to higher levels of development, regional inequalities tend to be narrowed down. In this contest it is worth mentioning the broad hypothesis of development suggested by Kuznets "that economic progress, measured by rising inequalities, but that these disparities ultimately go way as the benefits of development permeate more widely."[2]

The industrial development that took place in India prior to independence and sometime thereafter was unbalanced, as it was largely concentrated in a few states and within them in a few districts and cities. Consequently, regional imbalance has become one the of major policy issues for economists and planners since independence. Balanced regional development has, thus, become one of the central objectives of planning in India.

Balanced Regional Development of Industries

In process of economic development outcome is more important than the outlay. As such there is need for appropriate economic policies in order to ensure all-round economic development. According to Arthur Lewis "sound economic policies are more important to economic development than mere expenditure of money by the government".[3] No doubt it is important to establish industries in a planned economy. In order to create a climate for speedy development and acceleration of economic growth it is equally important to highlight the need for dispersal of industries on socio-economic and strategic grounds. In other words much more importance should be given to the regional development of the country, particularly in vast country like India which requires an overall development.

The principal objective of regional development is to promote industrial development, in order to ensure more and even development of the country. More specifically the objectives of regional development is to establish optimal industrial activity, basing on broader sociological, economic and strategically considerations. Incidentally regional development also aims at establishing at link between industrial activity and the heritage of the region. More importantly regional development aims at the distribution of employment opportunities on an equitable basis without letting the opportunities to confine only to a few regions of the state. Unless employment opportunities are equitable distributed to all the regions of the state, it may result increasing gaps in the per capita income among different regions.

These regional disparities in the distribution of income and wealth may even adversely affect national integration in the long run. Balanced regional development, besides achieving economic objectives, also aims to achieve certain social objectives which relate to the avoidance of emigration of labour and uplift of backward regions. Thus the central idea of the balanced regional development is to enrich the socio economic development of all the regions by stopping undesirable growth of agglomerations in particular regions.

Further, balanced development of all regions and all States in a country is necessary to draw the available human and material resources throughout the country into the development process and to enable people in all regions to share the benefits of development. According to the Planning commission, the balanced regional development has always been an essential component of the Indian development strategy in order to ensure the unity and integrity of the nation. Since not all parts of the country are equally well-endowed to take advantage of growth opportunities, and since historical inequalities have not been eliminated, planned intervention is required to ensure that large regional imbalances do not recur.

Incentives to Promote Investment in Backward Areas

Various incentives, both fiscal and otherwise, have been provided in order to tackle the problem of industrial backwardness and to promote private investment in backward areas. These incentives have been provided by the States and by public sector financial institutions.

State Government Incentives

State Governments have also offered incentives to attract private sector units to the backward regions. These incentives include provision of developed plots with power and water on a no-profit no-loss basis, exemption from payments of water charges for some years, interest-free loans on sales tax dues, exemption from Octroi duties, exemption from payment of property taxes for some years, preferential treatment for the purchase of stores for units located in backward areas, subsidy on industrial housing scheme etc. In recent years more than half the assistance sanctioned by SFCs, SIDCO and SIICs went to districts designated as backward for the concessional finance schemes.

Concessional Finance by Major Financial Institutions

The three major public sector financial institutions, viz., Industrial Development Bank of India (IDBI), the Industrial Finance Corporation of India (IFCI) and the Industrial Credit and Investment Corporation of India (ICICI) provide concessional finance for industrial projects located in backward areas. These concessions relate to a lower rate of interest on rupee loans (9.5 % as against 11.5 %), a longer period of repayment (generally 15 to 20 years, as against 10 to 12 years), participation in the risk capital or debenture issues, charging only half the normal rate of underwriting commission, waiving of commitment charges, etc.

The above three public sector financial institutions have also taken many other steps for the development of backward areas. They have prepared, at their own cost, feasibility study of projects which seem promising and encouraged prospective entrepreneurs. These institutions also run entrepreneurial training programmes for the benefit of small and medium entrepreneurs. The IDBI has been instrumental in setting up several technical consultancy organisations (TCOs) throughout the country. These organisations provided technical consultancy service, which is necessary for the development of backward areas.

SECTIONS II

The State of Andhra Pradesh consists of three geographic regions, namely, Costal Andhra, Telangana, and Rayalaseema. Of the three regions Telangana region has been identified as backward region. As such this region should recieve relatively higher amounts of financial assistances. As it has been the policy of the government to achieve balanced development of all regions, the APSFC is accepted to lay special emphasis on extending assistance to industrial units in the most back ward areas of the State.

In view of this an in depth analysis is made on of the role of APSFC in promoting balanced regional development in the state of Andhra Pradesh with particular reference to the three regions during the pre- and post-reform periods.

The new Industrial Policy announced by the Government of India in July 1991 is to be considered as a land-mark in industrial development of India. The main objectives of industrial policy are: (a) unshackle the Indian industrial economy from the cobwebs of unnecessary bureaucratic regulation, and (b) To introduce liberalization in order to integrate the Indian economy with world economy, as such a see change, in terms of liberalization has been taking place in the Indian economy. Hence, in order to examine the role of APSFC during period pre and post liberalization period, the year 1991 is taken as a bench-mark. Besides taking 1991 as the dividing line for the pre- and post-reform periods, a 15-year period ending with 1991 i.e. 1976-77 to 1990-91 is chosen the pre-reform period and a fifteen year period spreading over 1991-92 to 2005-06 is taken as the post-reform period.

Region-wise Sanctions of Term Loans during Pre-reform Period

The data relating to the region-wise sanctions of term loans during pre-reform period (1976-77 to 1990-91) are presented in Table 3.1. As can be seen from the table that Telangana region has been claiming a majority share in the sanction of term loans in all the years of the pre reform period with the

Table 3.1 : Region-wise Sanctions of Term Loans during Pre-Reofrm Period

(Amount in Rs. 000)

Year	Coastal Andhra	Rayalaseema	Telangana	Year-wise Total
1	2	3	4	5
1976-77	49824	12106	6563	68493
	(72.74)	(17.67)	(9.58)	(100.00)
1977-78	66356	33334	1036	100726
	(65.88)	(33.09)	(1.03)	(100.00)
1978-79	97878	49963	146273	294114
	(33.28)	(16.99)	(49.73)	(100.00)
1979-80	102779	61381	209705	373865
	(27.49)	(16.42)	(56.09)	(100.00)
1980-81	128868	74475	263421	466764
	(27.61)	(15.96)	(56.44)	(100.00)
1981-82	180304	77396	358247	615947
	(29.27)	(12.57)	(58.16)	(100.00)

1	2	3	4	5
1982-83	239659	92715	364075	696449
	(34.41)	(13.31)	(52.28)	(100.00)
1983-84	261230	96473	373169	730872
	(35.74)	(13.20)	(51.06)	(100.00)
1984-85	273488	109966	510126	893580
	(30.61)	(12.31)	(57.09)	(100.00)
1985-86	302053	175016	586818	1063887
	(28.39)	(16.45)	(55.16)	(100.00)
1986-87	297335	257752	770064	1325151
	(22.44)	(19.45)	(58.11)	(100.00)
1987-88	367431	244141	661644	1273216
	(28.86)	(19.18)	(51.97)	(100.00)
1988-89	366144	302321	969299	1637764
	(22.36)	(18.46)	(59.18)	(100.00)
1989-90	466466	316496	1067338	1850300
	(25.21)	(17.11)	(57.68)	(100.00)
1990-91	644267	434987	1386580	2465834
	(26.13)	(17.64)	(56.23)	(100.00)
Region Total	**3844082**	**2338522**	**7776979**	**13959583**
	(27.53)	**(16.75)**	**(56.72)**	**(100.00)**

Source: Annual Reports of APSFC.

Diagram 3.1 : Region-wise Sanction of during Pre-reform Period

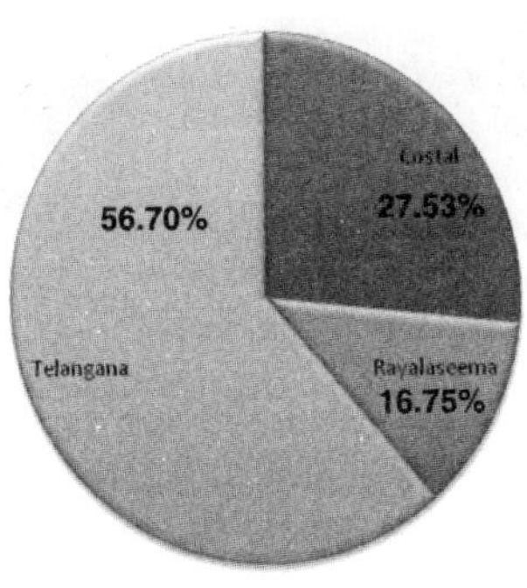

exception of 1976-77 and 1977-78. It is also interesting to note that in the overall pre reform period the total loans sanctioned by APSFC amounted to Rs 1395,95,83 crores. Of this total amount sanctioned the Telangana region claimed as high as 52.72 per cent, while coastal Andhra region obtained 27.53 percent followed Rayalaseema region with 16.75 per cent. Hence, it may be inferred from the above analysis that APSFC has been encouraging balanced regional development by sanctioning more term loans to most back ward region of Telangana.

Region-wise Sanctions of Term Loans during the Post-Reform Period

The statistical information relating to the region-wise sanctions of term loans during post-reform period (1991-92 to 2005-06) is presented in Table 3.2. During the post-reform period also Telangana region has secured major share in all the years without any exception. The total sanction made by APSFC to State amounted to Rs. 4214,49,53 crores. Out of the total term loans advanced, the Telangana region has obtained 60.04 per cent, while coastal Andhra region has received 28.60 per cent, followed Rayalaseema with a meager share of 11.36 per cent.

The figures in parentheses indicate percentages of total.

Table 3.2 : Region-wise Sanctions of Term Loans during Post-Reofrm Period

(Amount in Rs. 000)

Year	Coastal Andhra	Rayalaseema	Telangana	Year-wise Total
1	2	3	4	5
1991-92	577325 (28.08)	343156 (16.69)	1135524 (55.23)	2056005 (100.00)
1992-93	468317 (24.78)	250841 (13.27)	1170809 (61.95)	1889967 (100.00)
1993-94	326613 (34.72)	125217 (13.31)	488890 (51.97)	940720 (100.00)

1	2	3	4	5
1994-95	414096 (29.64)	202712 (14.51)	780283 (55.85)	1397091 (100.00)
1995-96	543941 (30.22)	285881 (15.88)	970293 (53.90)	1800115 (100.00)
1996-97	471719 (30.99)	200923 (13.20)	849429 (55.81)	1522071 (100.00)
1997-98	675743 (33.37)	223532 (11.04)	1125449 (55.59)	2024724 (100.00)
1998-99	733680 (27.33)	328797 (12.25)	1622244 (60.43)	2684721 (100.00)
1999-00	1057908 (31.56)	395400 (11.80)	1898590 (56.64)	3351898 (100.00)
2001-01	1037812 (26.48)	481020 (12.27)	2400272 (61.25)	3919104 (100.00)
2001-02	1004963 (25.76)	282183 (7.23)	2613426 (67.00)	3900572 (100.00)
2002-03	1023708 (26.60)	326994 (8.50)	2498090 (64.91)	3848792 (100.00)
2003-04	949777 (25.71)	347762 (9.41)	2397153 (64.88)	3694692 (100.00)
2004-05	1189762 (28.78)	539392 (13.05)	2404249 (58.17)	4133403 (100.00)
2005-06	1578512 (31.69)	455699 (9.15)	2946867 (59.16)	4981078 (100.00)
Region Total	**12053876 (28.60)**	**4789509 (11.36)**	**25301568 (60.04)**	**42144953 (100.00)**

Source : Annual Reports of APSFC.

Note : The figures in parentheses indicate percentages of total.

Diagram 3.2 : Region-wise Sanction of Term Loans during Pre-reform period

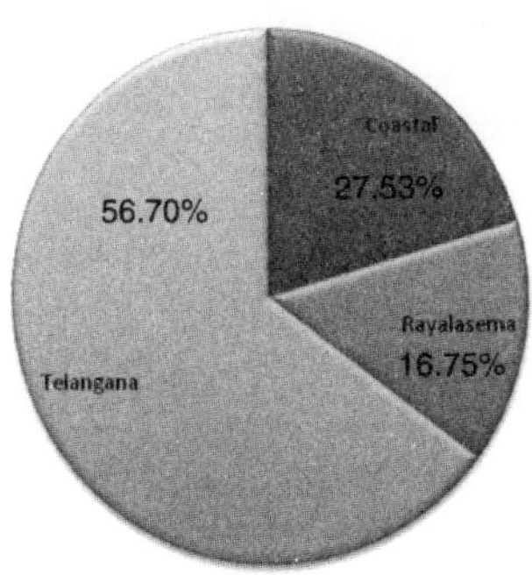

Region-wise Disbursements of Term Loans During Pre-reform Period

The data relating to the region-wise disbursements of term loans it is interesting to note that during pre- reforms period are presented in Table 3.3.

In respect the disbursements of terms loan also Telangana region claimed the highest percentage in the total disbursements of terms loans in all the years of pre-reforms period with the exception the years 1976-77. The share of Telangana region is amazingly as high as 91.29 per cent in the year 1982-83. It is evident from the table that out of the total disbursements of term loans made during the pre-reform period, a major share of 67.71 per cent is claimed by Telangana region, while 20.47 per cent went to Andhra region and 14.82 per cent went to Rayalaseema region.

Table 3.3 : Region-wise Disbursements of Term Loans during Pre-Reofrm Period

(Amount in Rs. 000)

Year	Coastal Andhra	Rayalaseema	Telangana	Year-wise Total
1	2	3	4	5
1976-77	16988	46456	20545	83989
	(20.23)	(55.31)	(24.46)	(100.00)
1977-78	13580	53086	191759	258425
	(5.25)	(20.54)	(74.20)	(100.00)
1978-79	56383	23658	80592	160633
	(35.10)	(14.73)	(50.17)	(100.00)
1979-80	87421	26763	143947	258131
	(33.87)	(10.37)	(55.77)	(100.00)
1980-81	92271	388991	1649221	2130483
	(4.33)	(18.26)	(77.41)	(100.00)

1	2	3	4	5
1981-82	115465	51918	204207	371590
	(31.07)	(13.97)	(54.95)	(100.00)
1982-83	162806	56758	2300851	2520415
	(6.46)	(2.25)	(91.29)	(100.00)
1983-84	145987	71083	256128	473198
	(30.85)	(15.02)	(54.13)	(100.00)
1984-85	196319	88152	301010	585481
	(33.53)	(15.06)	(51.41)	(100.00)
1985-86	212336	90250	353633	656219
	(32.36)	(13.75)	(53.89)	(100.00)
1986-87	206869	130728	45070	382667
	(54.06)	(34.16)	(11.78)	(100.00)
1987-88	261401	181602	547880	990883
	(26.38)	(18.33)	(55.29)	(100.00)
1988-89	312713	204242	584636	1101591
	(28.39)	(18.54)	(53.07)	(100.00)
1989-90	326986	216473	699499	1242958
	(26.31)	(17.42)	(56.28)	(100.00)
1990-91	375162	239373	787967	1402502
	(26.75)	(17.07)	(56.18)	(100.00)
Region Total	**2582687**	**1869533**	**8166945**	**12619165**
	(20.47)	**(14.82)**	**(64.71)**	**(100.00)**

Source: Annual Reports of APSFC

Note: The figures in parentheses indicate percentages to total.

Region-wise Disbursements of Term Loans During Post-reform Period

Region-wise disbursements of terms loan during the post-reforms period is shown in Table 3.4. It is observed from the table the share of Telangana region has reached a peak level of 82.82 per cent in the year 2005-06. It is also evident from the table that out of the total disbursements made during the post-reform period, a major share of 64.71 per cent is claimed by Telangana region, followed by Andhra region (20.47) and Rayalaseema region (14.82%). From the above analysis, it is clear that both in terms of sanctions as well as disbursements of term loans by APSFC, Telangana region accounted for the highest proportion of term loans followed by Coastal Andhra and Rayalaseema.

Table 3.4 : Region-wise Disbursements of Term Loans during Reform Period

(Amount in Rs. 000)

Year	Coastal Andhra	Rayalaseema	Telangana	Year-wise Total
1	2	3	4	5
1991-92	386547	268950	834186	1489683
	(25.95)	(18.05)	(56.00)	(100.00)
1992-93	329090	178376	754343	1261809
	(26.08)	(14.14)	(59.78)	(100.00)
1993-94	250329	113564	435570	799463
	(31.31)	(14.21)	(54.48)	(100.00)
1994-95	249802	130166	484100	864068
	(28.91)	(15.06)	(56.03)	(100.00)
1995-96	357733	177213	625888	1160834
	(30.82)	(15.27)	(53.92)	(100.00)
1996-97	333779	172699	615002	1121480
	(29.76)	(15.40)	(54.84)	(100.00)

1	2	3	4	5
1997-98	476460	184744	650100	1311304
	(36.33)	(14.09)	(49.58)	(100.00)
1998-99	508220	215812	897003	1621035
	(31.35)	(13.31)	(55.34)	(100.00)
1999-00	845588	311087	1485087	2641762
	(32.01)	(11.78)	(56.22)	(100.00)
2001-01	891288	322259	1614415	2827962
	(31.52)	(11.40)	(57.09)	(100.00)
2001-02	815187	299915	1969840	3084942
	(26.42)	(9.72)	(63.85)	(100.00)
2002-03	792804	242444	1974928	3010176
	(26.34)	(8.05)	(65.61)	(100.00)
2003-04	816087	229118	1786343	2831548
	(28.82)	(8.09)	(63.09)	(100.00)
2004-05	972604	404834	2107523	3484961
	(27.91)	(11.62)	(60.47)	(100.00)
2005-06	118942	421615	2605140	3145697
	(3.78)	(13.40)	(82.82)	(100.00)
Region Total	**2582687**	**1869533**	**8166945**	**12619165**
	(20.47)	**(14.82)**	**(64.71)**	**(100.00)**

Source : Annual Reports of APSFC

Note : The figures in parentheses indicate percentages to total

Number of Units Assisted by APSFC during the Pre-Reform Period

Table 3.5 shows the number of units assisted by the Corporation in Coastal Andhra, Rayalaseema and Telangana region in the State during pre-reform period. It can be seen from the table that while the total number of units assisted in the State by the corporation is 608 only in 1976-77, it went up to 9388 units during 1990-91.

Table 3.5 : Region-wise Number of Units Assisted by APSFC During Pre-Reform Period

(Amount in Rs. 000)

Year	Coastal Andhra	Rayalaseema	Telangana	Year-wise Total
1	2	3	4	5
1976-77	261 (42.93)	109 (17.93)	238 (39.14)	608 (100.00)
1977-78	425 (30.44)	289 (20.70)	682 (48.85)	1396 (100.00)
1978-79	482 (32.59)	353 (23.87)	644 (43.54)	1479 (100.00)
1979-80	530 (38.94)	214 (15.72)	617 (45.33)	1361 (100.00)
1980-81	1231 (50.93)	375 (15.52)	811 (33.55)	2417 (100.00)
1981-82	631 (33.78)	353 (18.90)	884 (47.32)	1868 (100.00)
1982-83	1794 (57.30)	504 (16.10)	833 (26.60)	3131 (100.00)
1983-84	729 (40.34)	371 (20.53)	707 (39.13)	1807 (100.00)
1984-85	649 (35.33)	408 (22.21)	780 (42.46)	1837 (100.00)
1985-86	784 (35.64)	562 (25.55)	854 (38.82)	2200 (100.00)
1986-87	780 (30.03)	757 (29.15)	1060 (40.82)	2597 (100.00)

1	2	3	4	5
1987-88	1009 (27.59)	1115 (30.49)	1533 (41.92)	3657 (100.00)
1988-89	949 (26.43)	1095 (30.49)	1547 (43.08)	3591 (100.00)
1989-90	1287 (23.36)	2342 (42.50)	1881 (34.14)	5510 (100.00)
1990-91	2802 (29.85)	2984 (31.79)	3602 (38.37)	9388 (100.00)
Region Total	**14343** **(33.47)**	**11831** **(27.61)**	**16673** **(39.91)**	**42847** **(100.00)**

Source : Annual Reports of APSFC

Note : The figures in parentheses indicate per centages to total.

The region-wise analysis reveled that while the number of units assisted in Coastal Andhra were 261units in 1976-77, this figure went up to 2802 during 1990-91. However, it can be observed that the share of this region has registered a downward trend barring few years. In the case of the Rayalaseema region, which secured assistance only 109 units in 1976-77, could secure assistance for as many as 2984 units by 1990-91. It can be observed that share of this region in the total number of units assisted by the APSFC has shown a steady increase indicating a rise from 17.92 per cent in 1976-77 to 31.78 per cent in 1990-91.

In Telangana region the number of units assisted by the APSFC stood at 238 units in 1976-77 while, the number of assisted units touched 3602 units during 1990-91. Telangana region has been also accounting for steady rise during pre-reform period. The overall picture pertaining to the number of units assisted by APSFC reveals that it is Telangana which is most favoured region followed by Costal Andhra and Rayalaseema Regions.

Number of Units Assisted by APSFC During Post-Reform Period

Table 3.6 reveals that number of units assisted by the APSFC during the post-reform period. It can be observed from the table that the number of assisted units to Coastal Andhra region stood at 1200 in 1991-92 while the number of units assisted during 2005-06 stood at 353. The total share of this region is 30 per cent which secured a total number of 7521 units during post-reform period.

Table 3.6 : Region-wise Number of Units Assisted by APSFC During Post Reform Period

(Amount in Rs. 000)

Year	Coastal Andhra	Rayalaseema	Telangana	Year wise Total
1	2	3	4	5
1991-92	1200	1412	2087	4699
	(25.54)	(30.05)	(44.41)	(100.00)
1992-93	1174	713	1502	3389
	(34.64)	(21.04)	(44.32)	(100.00)
1993-94	625	292	532	1449
	(43.13)	(20.15)	(36.71)	(100.00)
1994-95	441	280	485	1206
	(36.57)	(23.22)	(40.22)	(100.00)
1995-96	377	369	571	1317
	(28.63)	(28.02)	(43.36)	(100.00)
1996-97	316	274	570	1160
	(27.24)	(23.62)	(49.14)	(100.00)
1997-98	394	241	635	1270
	(31.02)	(18.98)	(50.00)	(100.00)

1	2	3	4	5
1998-99	348	224	693	1265
	(27.51)	(17.71)	(54.78)	(100.00)
1999-00	451	366	914	1731
	(26.05)	(21.14)	(52.80)	(100.00)
2001-01	477	392	855	1724
	(27.67)	(22.74)	(49.59)	(100.00)
2001-02	402	215	736	1353
	(29.71)	(15.89)	(54.40)	(100.00)
2002-03	331	187	728	1246
	(26.57)	(15.01)	(58.43)	(100.00)
2003-04	331	148	674	1153
	(28.71)	(12.84)	(58.46)	(100.00)
2004-05	301	173	587	1061
	(28.37)	(16.31)	(55.33)	(100.00)
2005-06	353	156	534	1043
	(33.84)	(14.96)	(51.20)	(100.00)
RegionTotal	**7521**	**5442**	**12103**	**25066**
	(30.00)	**(21.72)**	**(48.28)**	**(100.00)**

Source : Annual Reports of APSFC

Note : The figures in parentheses indicate percentages to total.

In respect of Rayalaseema region the number of total units assisted by APSFC is 5442 accounting for 21.72 per cent. In this region also while the number of assisted units stood at 1412 in 1991-92 this went down to 156 in 2005-06. The total share of this region is 21.72 per cent during the post reform period. Though in Telangana region the number of sanctioned units registered was 2087 in 1991-92, this went down to 534 in 2005-06. The total number of loans assisted by the corporation stood at 12103, constituting 48.28 of total number of units in the State during the same period. Thus the share of this region has almost claimed 50 per cent of the total loans sanctioned to the number of units in the state of Andhra Pradesh.

From Tables 3.5 and 3.6 it can be concluded that as regards the number of units assisted, the share of Rayalaseema declined from 27.6 per cent in pre reform period to 21.72 per cent in post reform period. While Telangana region secured an increasing share i.e. from 39.91 per cent in pre-reform period to 48.28 per cent. In the case of Costal Andhra region, the share of the total number of units assisted went down from 33.47 per cent in pre-reform period to 30 per cent in post reform period. Thus, it is observed that while Telangana region received increased tinanancial support from APSFC, costal Andhra and Rayalaseema regions received relatively less financial support over the study period.

The measurement of regional dispersal of the Corporation's financing in terms of sanctions and disbursements during pre- and post-reform periods is attempted by computing Herfindal Index, in the identified three regions of the sate the results are presented in Table 3.7. In terms of sanctions the Herfindal Index was recorded 0.57 in case of disbursements it is registered 0.42 in 1990-91. It is also seen from the table with respect to disbursements the index was 0.44 in 1976-77 which decreased to 0.42. Similar analysis has been made in post- reform period. In terms of sanctions the index was 0.41 in 1991-92 it went up to 0.46 by 2005-06. In case of disbursements the index is 0.41 in 1991-91 and it is significantly increased to 0.71 by 2005-06. From the Herfindhal index, it is observed that on the whole the degree of dispersal of sanctions and disbursements are more during the end of the post-reform period.

Table 3.7 : Diversification of Sacntions and Disbursements at the Beginning and End of the Pre-, Post-Reform Period

(Rs. crores)

Year	1976-77				1990-91			
Region	Sanctions		Disburse-ments		Sanctions		Disburse-ments	
Coastal	4.98	24.8004	1.1	1.21	64.43	4151.225	37.52	1407.75
Rayalaseema	1.21	1.4641	4.65	21.6225	43.5	1892.25	23.94	573.1236
Telangana	0.66	0.4356	2.05	4.2025	138.66	19226.6	7.88	62.0944
Total	6.85	26.7001	7.8	27.035	246.59	25270.07	69.34	2042.968
		46.9225		60.84		60806.63		4808.036
		0.57		**0.44**		**0.42**		**0.42**
Year	**1991-92**				**2005-06**			
Region	**Sanctions**		**Disburse-ments**		**Sanctions**		**Disburse-ments**	
Coastal	57.73	3332.753	38.65	1493.823	157.85	24916.62	11.89	141.3721
Rayalaseema	34.32	1177.862	26.9	723.61	45.57	2076.625	42.16	1777.466
Telangana	113.55	12893.6	83.42	6958.896	294.69	86842.2	260.51	67865.46
Total	205.6	17404.22	148.97	9176.329	498.11	113835.4	314.56	69784.3
		42271.36		22192.06		248113.6		98947.99
		0.41		**0.41**		**0.46**		**0.71**

Herfindhal index = $\sum x^2/\sum x^2$

Source: Annual Reports of APSFC.

SECTION III

In order to get clearer insights into balanced regional development, an attempt is made in this section to study the operation of Branches of APSFC in the districts of each region in the State of Andhra Pradesh and to analyze the sanctioned amounts in each district.

Expansion of Branches

Initially the APSFC has opened three Braches at Hyderabad, Nizamabad and Kurnool during the year 1976-77. One-man branches at Nizamabad and Kurnool were converted into full-fledged branches. In the same year three more one-man branches have been opened at Nalgonda, Khammam and Kakinada. The corporation has also opened two new branches at Rajahamundry and Khammam. In addition to these it has opened five new representative offices at Rangareddy, Guntur, Cuddapah, Tirupathi, and Karimnagar making the total number of representative offices to 10 in the same year.

In order to render better service to the clients, especially to the marginal entrepreneurs, the corporation has opened three new branches at Nellore, Guntur and Anantapur during the year 1980-81, making the total number of branches to 12. It has also opened one more field office at Nalgonda taking the total number of field offices to eight. In the year 1982-83, a policy decision has been taken by the Corporation to open three more Branch offices in the state to further hasten the process of assistance.

During the year 1985-86 the corporation has taken the policy decision to further decentralize its operations by opening four more branches in the districts of Mahabubnagar, Vizianagaram, Prakasam and Medak in the State by upgrading the existing field offices. The corporation during the financial year 1992-93 categorized the 23 branches into four broad groups in term of funds required for their operations and stipulated ceiling on their maximum holdings. This was adopted to ensure better financial discipline and the branches were required to transfer the excess balances on weekly basis to head offices central pool. The steps taken in this direction yielded better results in the monitoring of funds and at the same time the branches that require funds to meet commitments on hand also received funds adequately. The branches and the field offices have started rendering good services for the speedy development of industries in the State especially in the small scale and tiny sector units, located in rural and backward areas.

The Corporation activities have been organized basically at three levels, at the State level at district, level and finally at field office. The decision-making process has been decentralized through powers of delegation of sanction and recoveries to the managing director and general managers who are empowered to disburse all the loans sanctioned by various authorities. For operational convenience of the APSFC, all the districts in the state were divided into five zones. Of the total five zones, Hyderabad zone covers the districts of Hyderabad, Medak, Rangareddy and Mahabubnagar, while Vijayawada zone comprises the districts of Krishna, Khammam, Guntur, and Prakasam. On the other hand Tirupati zone consists of Chittoor, Cuddapah, Anantapur, Nellore and Kurnool districts. While Visakhapatnam zone has the jurisdiction over the districts of Visakhapatnam, Srikakulam, East Godavari and West Godavari and Vizianagaram, Warangal zone consists of Warangal, Nizamabad, Adilabad and Karimnagar districts.

District-wise Analysis of Backward Districts

In order to study the role of APSFC in extending sanctions with particular reference to identified backward districts of Andhra Pradesh, the following methodology is adopted. For operational convenience, the assistance sanctioned to the number of units by the APSFC, during three decadal points of time i.e. 1981-82, 1991-92, and 2001-02 are selected. For these three points of time, the average assistance sanctioned is arrived at by dividing the total assistance with the number of districts in the state of Andhra Pradesh. After arriving average assistance sanctioned by APSFC, an hypothesis is formulated. That is to say the districts which are considered officially backward districts are expected to get comparatively more assistance than the average assistance of the State. Similarly the districts which are considered as forward districts are expected to get assistance less than the State average. The statistical information relating to the sanctions made to the backward districts by APSFC are presented in Table 3.8. The state average of sanctions made by APSFC is worked out to be Rs. 30258.57 crores in the year 1981-82. However the data reveal that the backward districts, which were not able to get even the sanctions level to the average sanctioned loan of the State, are Adilabad, Karimnagar, Nalgonda, Warangal, Nizamabad, Kurnool, Mahabubnagar, Anantapur, Kadapa, Nellore, Khammam Prakasam, and Srikakulam. There are only two backward districts, namely Medak and Chittoor, which are able to get more than the average sanctioned loan.

With regard to the time period 1991-92 the State average is worked out to be Rs. 89391.52 crores. from the data it clear that the backward districts such as Karimnagar, Warangal, Nizamabad, Kurnool, Mahabubnagar, Anantapur, Kadapa, Nellore, Khammam, Prakasam, and Srikakulam were not able to secure the average sanctioned loan of the sate. On the other the backward districts like Nalgonda, Medak, and Chittoor could get more than the average sanctioned loan.

In the year 2001-02, the state average is worked out to be Rs.13,4127.9 crores. It is observed from the table that the following backward districts were not able to get even that average amount of sanctioned from to the state. These included Karimnagar, Warangal, Nizamabad, Kurnool, Mahabubnagar, Anantapur, Chittoor, Kadapa, Khammam, Prakasam, and Srikakulam. There were only four backward districts namely Nalgonda, Medak, Mahabubnagar and Nellore, which were able to get more than the average sanctioned loan. From this analysis it is clear that most of the

Table 3.8 : Trends in Sanctions and Number of Units to the Backward Districts

(Amount in Rs. 000)

Year	1981-82		1991-92		2001-02	
Districts	Sanctions	Num of Units	Sanctions	Num of Units	Sanctions	Num of Unit
Adilabad	8298 (3.01)	43	NA	NA	NA	NA
Kariamnagar	9646 (3.50)	37	80002 (7.22)	412	46645 (2.86)	23
Nalgonda	19319 (7.02)	32	174801 (15.77)	388	246831 (15.14)	68
Warangal	18923 (6.87)	40	61093 (5.51)	174	125165 (7.68)	56
Nizamabad	116294 (4.22)	68	39348 (3.55)	52	36785 (2.26)	36
Medak	71920 (26.12)	108	138235 (12.47)	140	256450 (15.73)	82
Kurnool	19443 (7.0)	80	73404 (6.62)	367	60856 (3.73)	50
Mahaboobnagar	17705 (6.43)	.35	44381 (4.00)	120	160744 (9.86)	59
Anathapur	15064 (5.47)	84	74991 (6.77)	364	50750 (3.11)	38
Chittoor	31744 (11.53)	132	138035 (12.46)	452	115789 (7.10)	89
Kadapa	11145 (4.05)	57	56726 (5.12)	229	54788 (3.36)	38
Nellore	10194 (3.70)	43	69533 (6.27)	161	188476 (11.56)	82
Khammam	9376 (3.41)	43	73446 (6.63)	137	104015 (6.38)	43
Prakasam	13327 (4.84)	51	5177 (14.67)	115	87543 (5.37)	66
Srikakulam	7607 (2.76)	38	32456 (2.93)	66	95572 (5.86)	50
Total	275340	891	1108222	3177	1630409	780
Total Ap	695947		2056005		3900572	
State Average	30258.57		89391.52		134127.9	

Source : Annual Reports of APSFC

Note : The figures in parentheses indicate per centages to total.

backward districts are getting lesser assistances when compared to the state average by the APSFC. During the three decadal points of time under consideration.

District-wise Analysis of Forward Districts

Similar methodology is adopted to identify those forward districts which have received more than the average sanctioned assistance of the State by the APSFC for the three selected years. It may be observed from the table 3.9 in the

Table 3.9 : District wise Classification of Term Loans Sanctioned to Forwed Districts During the Year 1981-82, 1991-92, 2001-02

(Amount in Rs. 000)

YEAR	1981-82		1991-92		2001-02	
DISTRICTS	Sanctions	Num of Units	Sanctions	Num of Units	Sanctions	Num of Unit
Hyderabad	191431 (56.70)	490	117448 (12.60)	208	632947 (28.58)	145
Rangareddy	NA	NA	391320 (41.97)	416	948615 (42.83)	184
Guntur	24420 (7.17)	87	78800 (8.45)	254	111145 (5.02)	43
Krishna	35212 (10.31)	144	144179 (15.46)	267	146248 (6.60)	39
West Godavari	26231 (7.70)	47	40677 (4.36)	100	120542 (5.44)	27
East Godavari	19660 (5.77)	58	85620 (4.17)	78	109326 (4.94)	24
Visakhapatnam	43744 (12.84)	163	58444 (6.27)	125	97050 (4.38)	38
Vizianagaram	NA	NA	15845 (1.70)	34	49061 (2.22)	33
Total	316999 (100)	989	932333 (100)	1482	2214934 (100)	533
Total Ap	615947	1868	2056005	4699	3900572	1353
State Average	30258.57		89391.52		134127.9	

Source : Annual Reports of APSFC

Note : The figures in parentheses indicate per centages to total.

year 1981-82, the only two forward districts, viz., Hyderabad and Visakhapatnam have received more that the state average.

However, in the year 1991-92, Hyderabad, Rangareddy, and Krishna, are the only three districts which obtained more than average sanctioned amount. Similarly in the next point of time, i.e in the year 2001-02, Hyderabad and Rangareddy were the only two districts which received more than the state average, sanctioned by APSFC. From this it may be observed that most of the forward districts in the state viz. Guntur, West Godavari, East Godavari, and Vizianagaram were getting less than average amount sanctioned in the respective years. Thus, similar to most of the backward districts, several forward districts were also getting relatively less assistance compared to the state average from the APSFC.

The above analysis of the role of APSFC in balanced regional development indicates that though the APSFC has been playing a vital role it has to play a more vital role in creation of a climate for speedy development and also acceleration of balanced regional development. In the next chapter an attempt is made to focus light on the assistance made by the APSFC to the small scale units, medium scale units along with the analysis of purpose-wise assistance extended by the Corporation

REFERENCES

1. Friedmann john and Alonso Williams (Eds.) *Regional development and Planning*, the MIT Press, Cambridge, 1967, p.3.
2. Debraj Ray, *Development Economics*, Oxford University Press, New Delhi, 2001, p. 199.
3. W. Arthur Lewis, *Development Planning in Practice – Leading Issues in Development Economics*, Ed. Gerald M. Meier, Oxford University Press, New York, 1964, p. 523.
4. Datt and sundram, *Indian Economy* S.Chand Company New Delhi, 2004, pp. 467-468.

CHAPTER

APSFC Assistance to Industrial Units

Introduction

The principal objectives spelt out by the Indian government on the eve of Independence included the acceleration of economic development, expansion of opportunities for gainful employment and progressive reduction of inequalities in our country. It is believed that promotion of small scale industries would facilitate realization of these objectives to a greater extent in the Indian context. Accordingly, the Indian industrial policy laid down a strong foundation for the development of small scale industries (SSIs) in the Indian economy.

One of the salient features of the Industrial Policy Resolution, 1956 clearly stated the need for encouraging the village and small industries. However, the Industrial Policy Statement of 1977 announced by the government is considered as a landmark in the history of small scale industry in India. Some of the features of this policy are worth mentioning here. The industrial policy statement believed that whatever that could be produced by the cottage industry should not be kept open for small-scale and large scale industries, similarly what ever output that could be produced by the small-scale sector, should not be produced by large scale industries. With a view to protect the small scale industries the policy statement made it clear that the then existing foreign collaborations will not be renewed in areas, where foreign technology know how is not needed. This policy also proposed to set up District Industries Centres in each district with the intention of providing all the necessary services and support needed by the small and village entrepreneurs. Most importantly, the policy aimed at making the available loanable funds of the public sector financial institutions largely for the small scale sector. Thus, with the encouragement given by the government from time to time, the small scale sector has grown to occupy a prominent place in the Indian economy.

This sector accounts for 40 per cent of the gross net over of the manufacturing sector, about 45 per cent of the manufacturing export, and about 35 per cent of the total exports of India. The employment in this sector is around 17.2 million in 2004-05, this contribution is next only to agriculture sector.

The SSI sector in India has been exhibiting an impressive performance in terms of exports and employment. The exports of SSI in 1973-74 accounted for Rs. 393 crores, claiming a share of 15.58 pre cent in total exports. In 1991-91 the exports of SSI sector rose to Rs. 9,5664 crores and has increased to Rs. 43,946 crores in 1997-98. The figures of Exports for the year 1998-99 and 2000-01 are Rs. 48,979 crores and Rs. 54,200.47 crores respectively. In 2004-05 the exports increased to Rs. 1,24,417 accounting for 27.41 percent in the total exports. While the total number of persons employed in the SSI sector was 39.70 lakhs in 1973-74, the number rose to 282.6 lakhs by 2004-05.

As such, the Small-Scale Industry has been staying in the Indian Economy as a potent instrument for accelerating the economic growth, providing employment to a larger number of people and earning substantial exports. Hence, the SSI units need to be shown greater concern to sustain its glorious role in the years to come. In this context it is proposed to study the role of APSFC in the promotion of SSIs units vis-a-vis medium scale units (MSIs) units. In order to have an over view of the APSFC's assistance to industrial units, an attempted is made in Section I to analyse the sanctions and disbursements made by APSFC to industries in Andhra Pradesh. In Section II constitution-wise assistance extended by APSFC is attempted. In Section III, APSFC's contribution to SSI and MSI is analyzed. To make an indepth analysis, the study period i.e. 1976-77 to 2005-06 is sub-divided into pre-reform period and post-reform period. The pre-reform period is taken to be 15 years earlier to starting of reforms and the post-reform period refers to the next 15 years commencing from the reforms. As such the pre-reform period is selected to be 1976-77 to 1990-91 and the post-reform period is taken to be 1991-92 to 2005-2006.

SECTION I

INDUSTRY- WISE SANCTIONS DURING PRE-REFORM PERIOD

The Corporation extends financial assistance for a wide variety of industrial products and services which are presented in Table 4.1. The table depicts that the corporation accorded the highest priority to the promotion of small scale and tiny sector industries through sanctions and disbursements. From the sanctions made since 1976-77 to the end of the March 1991, it is observed that the total annual sanctions for all industries increased from Rs. 135,921 lakhs during 1976-77 to Rs. 23,26,819 lakhs.

The industrial-wise analysis of loan assistance sanctioned by the corporation during the pre-reform period revealed the following: The chemical products industry occupied the first position by claiming an average amount of Rs. 244,49,353 lakhs accounting for 24.18 per cent of the total sanctions with total units 2339. Chemical industry is followed by services with an average amount of Rs. 125,03,293 lakhs accounting for 12.35 per cent of total sanctions.

The sanctions of this industry increased from Rs. 13,193 lakhs during 1976-77 to Rs. 431,197 lakhs by 1990-91, with total 3335 units. The food industry and non-metallic industry products on the other hand occupied third and fourth ranks

Table 4.1 : Industry-wise Sanctions in Pre-reform Period

(Amount in Rs. Lakhs)

Industry/Year	1975-76	1990-91	Total	AVG Amount
1	2	3	4	5
Food products	28322	312816	1673127	
	(1.69)	(18.70)	(100.00)	
Number of units	367	1171	7222	111541.48
Beverage& tobacco	1785	11737	125775	
	(1.42)	(9.33)	(100.00)	
Number of units	3	21	286	8385
Textiles	7414	220076	817152	
	(0.91)	(26.93)	(100.00)	
Number of units	1	2891	6185	54476.8
Wood products	992	28107	96938	
	(1.02)	(28.99)	(100.00)	
Number of units	51	351	1451	6462.53
Paper& paper products	4346	52056	314802	
	(1.38)	(16.54)	(100.00)	
Number of units	52	129	639	20986.8
Printing and publishing	2281	64195	322880	
	(0.71)	(19.88)	(100.00)	
Number of units	19	317	1547	21525.33
Leather products	238	21972	170188	
	(0.14)	(12.91)	(100.00)	
	73	310	636	11345.33
Rubber products	2189	44274	362386	
	(0.60)	(12.22)	(100.00)	
Number of Units	0	165	611	24159.06
Chemical products	32136	268090	3667403	
	(0.88)	(7.31)	(100.00)	
Number of Units	68	327	2339	244493.53
Non-metallic products	10748	406873	1517714	
	(0.71)	(26.81)	(100.00)	
Number of Units	73	658	3925	101180.93

(Contd. ...)

1	2	3	4	5
Transports vechiles &	1412	4962	89516	
spareparts	(1.58)	(5.54)	(100.00)	
Number of Units	7	16	154	5967.73
Petroleum products	0	23811	34419	
	0	(69.18)	(100.00)	
Number of Units	0	86	114	2294.6
Basic metal industry	9658	42924	458292	
	(2.11)	(9.37)	(100.00	
Number of Units	17	55	550	30552.8
Metal products	5020	45553	373704	
	(1.34)	(12.19)	(100.00)	
Number of Units	56	194	955	24913.6
Machinery	3944	103825	751270	
	(0.52)	(13.82)	(100.00)	
Number of Units	102	182	2084	50084.66
Electrical machinery	3944	44885	531540	
	(0.74)	(8.44)	(100.00	
Number of Units	18	99	697	35436
Miscellaneous	8299	85055	1445224	
manufacturing	(0.57)	(5.89)	(100.00	
Number of Units	98	461	2814	96348.26
Gas manufacturing	0	462	55207	
	0	(0.84)	(100.00)	
Number of Units	4	2	36	3680.46
Medical loans	0	102591	198783	
	0	(51.61)	(100.00)	
Number of Units	0	106	175	13252.2
Fishers loans	0	0	1428	
	0			
Number of Units	0	0	1680	95.2
Electricity generation supply	0	3241	8066	
	0	(40.18)	(100.00)	
Number of Units	0	17	48	537.73

1	2	3	4	5
Services	13193	431197	1875494	
	(0.70)	(22.99)	(100.00)	
Number of Units	10	1270	3335	125032.93
Other industries	0	8147	270441	
	0	(3.02)	(100.00)	
Number of Units	0	441	859	18029.4
Total	135921	2326819	15161749	

Source: Various Annual Repots of APSFC
Note: The figures in parentheses indicates percentages to total.

respectively. The food industry accounted average amount of Rs. 111,54,1.48 lakhs. The sanctions of food industry increased from Rs. 28,322 lakhs (1.69%) in 1976 to Rs. 312,816 lakhs (18.70%) by 1990-91 with total number of 7222 units. The non-metallic industry is accounted for average amount of Rs. 101,18,0.93 l lakhs. The Sanctions to this industry increased from Rs. 10,748 lakhs (0.71%) to Rs. 406,873 lakhs (26.81%). The Miscellaneous Manufacturing Industry accounted for an average amount of Rs. 96,34,8.26 lakhs with a total number of 2814 units. The sanctions to this industry increased from Rs. 8,299 lakhs (0.57%) to Rs. 85,055 lakhs (5.89%),Textiles industry which claimed an average amount Rs. 544,76.8 lakhs with total number of 6185 units. The Textiles industry sanctions increased significantly from Rs. 7,414 lakhs (0.91%) to Rs. 220,076 lakhs (26.93%).The machinery industry received an average amount of Rs. 50,08,4.66 lakhs with a total 2084 units. The sanctions obtained by machinery industry, increased from Rs. 3,944 lakhs (0.52%) to Rs. 103,825 (13.82%) lakhs in pre -reform period.

Basic Metal Industry, with total number of 550 units obtained an average amount of Rs. 305,52.8 lakhs. The sanctions to the Basic Metal Industry increased from Rs. 9,658 lakhs (2.11%) to Rs. 42,924 lakhs (9.37%).The Electrical Machinery Industry accounts for Rs. 35,436 lakhs, spreading over 697 units. The sanctions rose from Rs. 3,944 lakhs (0.74%)

to Rs. 44,885 lakhs (8.44%). The Electrical Machinery Industry is followed by Metal Products Industry with an average amount of Rs. 249,13.6 lakhs spreading over 955 units. Rubber products, Printing and Publishing, Paper and Paper products, Other industries, Medical loans, Leather products, Beverage and Tobacco industry, Wood products industries have also obtained reasonable financial support from the Corporation during the pre-reform period.

However, the Corporation sanctioned only a meagre amounts on an average to the Fisheries, Electricity Generation Supply, Petroleum Products, and Gas Manufacturing Industries. The fisheries industry with a total number of 1680 units obtained an amount of Rs. 95.2 lakhs. Electricity generation supply industry accounted for an average amount of Rs. 53,7.73 lakhs with 48 units. Petroleum Products Industry claimed an average amount of Rs. 22,94.6 lakhs with total number of 114 units during the same period.

Industry-wise Disbursements during Pre-reform Period

The data pertaining to industry-wise disbursements during the pre-reform period are presented in Table 4.2. From the data it may be observed that in terms of disbursements also same ranks with slight changes were obtained by the industries. It is heartening to note that service industry accounted for the highest average amount of Rs. 246,41,7.53 lakhs as disbursements from APSFC. The disbursements of service industry increased from Rs. 2,560 lakhs (0.07%) in 1976-77 to Rs. 29,19,661 lakhs (78.98%) by 1991-91. Chemical industry secured second place with average amount of Rs. 83,63,8.06 lakhs. The disbursements to chemical industry increased from Rs. 13,533 lakhs (1.08%) in 1976-77 to Rs. 213,462 lakhs (17.01%) lakhs by 1990-91 followed by food products industry with an average amount of Rs. 72,86,8.33 lakhs. Disbursements to this increased from Rs. 10,842 lakhs (0.99%) to Rs. 177,861 lakhs (16.27%) by 1990-91. Non-metallic industry obtained an average amount of Rs. 405,94.8 lakhs. The disbursements to this industry increased from Rs. 5,523 lakhs (0.91 %) in 1976-77 to Rs. 11,195 lakhs (1.83 %) by 1990-91. Textiles industry received an average amount of Rs. 544,76.8 lakhs. The disbursements to it increased from Rs. 5,139 lakhs (0.98 %) in 1976-77 to Rs. 96,950 lakhs (18.47 %) by 1990-91. Textiles industry is followed by Rubber Industry with total average disbursements of Rs. 30,90,5.73 lakhs. The industry's disbursements increased from Rs. 753 lakhs (0.16 %) to Rs. 292,88 lakhs (6.31 %). It is heartening to note that the total units increased from 0 to 165 units during the same period.

On the disbursements front also textiles, Fisheries, Electricity Generation Supply, Petroleum Products, Transport Vehicles and spare parts received very meagre amounts of disbursements during this period.

Table 4.2 : Industry-wise Disbursements in Pre-Reform Period

(Amount in Rs. Lakhs)

Industry/Year	1976-77	1990-91	Total	AVG Amount
1	2	3	4	5
Food products	10842	177861	1093025	
	(0.99)	(16.27)	(100.00)	
Number of Units	367	1171	7222	72868.33
Beverage& tobacco	859	6717	119087	
	(0.72)	(5.64)	(100.00)	
Number of Units	3	21	286	7939.13
Textiles	5139	96950	524727	
	(0.98)	(18.48)	(100.00)	
Number of Units	1	2891	6185	3498.18
Wood products	785	9138	97287	
	(0.81)	(9.39)	(100.00)	
Number of Units	51	351	1451	6485.85
Paper & paper products	6598	25106	189800	
	(3.48)	(13.23)	(100.00)	
Number of Units	52	129	639	12653.33

(Contd. ...)

1	2	3	4	5
Printing and publishing	1132	48528	186117	
	(0.61)	(26.07)	(100.00)	
Number of Units	19	317	1547	124078
Leather products	49	13798	93162	
	(0.05)	(14.81)	(100.00)	
Number of Units	73	310	636	6210.8
Rubber products	753	29288	463586	
	(0.16)	(6.318)	(100.00)	
Number of Units	0	165	611	30905.73
Chemical products	13533	213462	1254571	
	(1.08)	(17.01)	(100.00)	
Number of Units	68	327	2339	83638.06
Non-metallic products	5523	11195	608922	
	(0.91)	(1.84)	(100.00)	
Number of Units	73	658	3925	40594.8
Transports vechiles	1194	4287	58884	
& spareparts	(2.03)	(7.28)	(100.00)	
Number of Units	7	16	154	3925.6
Petroleum products	23	4421	14737	
	(0.16)	(30.00)	(100.00)	
Number of Units	0	86	114	982.46
Basic metal industry	7995	49626	330842	
	(2.42)	(15.00)	(100.00)	
Number of Units	17	55	550	22056.13
Metal products	3852	22603	233316	
	(1.65)	(9.69)	(100.00)	
Number of Units	56	194	955	15554.4
Machinery	6791	39387	453494	
	(1.50)	(8.69)	(100.00)	
Number of Units	102	182	2084	30232.9

1	2	3	4	5
Electrical machinery	2395	21220	320462	
	(0.75)	(6.62)	(100.00)	
Number of Units	102	182	2084	213660.13
Miscellaneous	1947	83342	392397	
manufacturing	(0.50)	(21.24)	(100.00)	
Number of Units	98	461	2814	26159.8
Gas manufacturing	1081	766	68950	
	(1.57)	(1.11)	(100.00)	
Number of Units	4	2	36	4596.66
Medical loans	0	57757	94503	
	0	(61.12)	(100.00)	
Number of Units	0	106	175	6300.2
Fishers loans	0	0	1428	
	0	0	(100.00)	
Number of Units	0	0	1680	95.2
Electricity generation supply	0	1528	8710	
	0	(17.54)	(100.00)	
Number of Units	0	17	48	580.66
Services	2560	2919661	3696263	
	(0.07)	(78.99)	(100.00)	
Number of Units	10	1270	3335	246417.53
Other industries	0	52843	163747	
	0	(32.27)	(100.00)	
Number of Units	0	441	859	10916.46
Total	72276	3880346	10468017	

Source: Various Annual Repots of APSFC

Note: The figures in parentheses indicates percentages to total.

Industry-wise Sanctions During the Post-Reform Period

The industrial production in the State of Andhra Pradesh significantly increased during the post-reform period due to better industrial relations, easy availability of essential raw materials, improved power supply coupled with various incentives being given both by the state and the central governments in order to accelerated growth of industrial development. On the other hand, there has been a marked decline in food production due to cyclones and heavy rain fall in some districts and prolonged dry spell in some other districts. Some groups of industries like textiles, electrical, general engineering etc., have faced the problem of slackening demand and resultant accumulation of investors. It is in this background, the assistance extended by the APSFC to the industrial units under various categories of industries during post-reform period is analyzed below.

Data relating to the industry-wise loan assistance sanctioned by the Corporation are presented in the table-4.3. As can be seen from the table, Food Products accounted for a highest proportion of loan assistance with an average amount of Rs. 635,87,4.93 lakhs covering 3258 units. However, The sanctions decreased from 38.44 per cent in 1991-92 to 4.98 percent by 2005-06. It is disheartening to note that the number of units also registered a decreasing trend year after year. Food industry is followed by 'Other Industries' taking an average amount of Rs. 532,00,9.67 lakhs in the total disbursements. The sanctions rose from Rs. 65,004 lakhs (0.8 %) in 1991-92 to Rs. 14,05,136 lakhs (17.61%) in 2005-06. Chemical Industry stood at third position with an average amount of Rs. 296,17,9.87 lakhs consisting of 1678 units. The sanctions of chemical industry significantly increased from Rs. 223,042 lakhs (5.02%) to Rs. 302,376 lakhs (6.81%) during this period. Chemical industry is followed by Textiles with an average amount of Rs. 233,01,5.67 lakhs consisting of total 842 units. Services Industry comes next with an average amount of Rs. 208,97,6.47 lakhs with 4683 units. However the sanctions decreased from Rs. 309,988 lakhs (9.89%)

Table 4.3 : Industry-wise Sanctions in Post-Reform Period

(Amount in Rs. Lakhs)

Industry/Year	1976-77	1990-91	Total	AVG Amount
1	2	3	4	5
Food products	366298	475194	9538124	
	(38.44)	(4.98)	(100.00)	
Number of Units	713	131	3258	635874.93
Beverage& tobacco	291	40251	595345	
	(0.05)	(6.76)	(100.00)	
Number of Units	1	15	174	39689.67
Textiles	170035	365386	3495235	
	(4.86)	(10.45)	(100.00)	
Number of Units	274	20	1842	233015.67
Wood products	12835	10389	185611	
	(6.91)	(5.60)	(100.00)	
Number of Units	144	20	433	12374.07
Paper& paper products	501701	15721	1318371	
	(38.05)	(1.19)	(100.00)	
Number of Units	86	20	434	87891.4
Printing and publishing	35729	39835	470784	
	(7.59)	(8.46)	(100.00)	
Number of Units	117	5	386	31385.6
Leather products	27770	0	185857	
	(14.94)	(0.00)	(100.00)	
Number of Units	107	7	172	12390.47
Rubber products	37625	851325	1884804	
	(2.00)	45.17	100	
Number of Units	71	0	294	125653.6
Chemical products	223042	302376	4442698	
	(5.02)	(6.81)	(100.00)	
Number of Units	150	99	1678	296179.87
Non-metallic products	226567	11503	1718473	
	(13.18)	(0.67)	(100.00)	
Number of Units	402	127	2328	9230.13
Transports vechiles &	24227	0	138452	
spareparts	(17.50)	(0.00)	(100.00)	
Number of Units	14	4	106	114564.87

(Contd. ...)

1	2	3	4	5
Petroleum products	21968	264607	1095989	
	(2.00)	(24.14)	(100.00)	
Number of Units	62	0	132	73065.13
Basic metal industry	53362	71281	965200	
	(5.53)	(7.39)	(100.00)	
Number of Units	35	23	426	64346.67
Metal products	34780	113353	1155937	
	(3.01)	(9.81)	(100.00)	
Number of Units	94	20	614	77062.47
Machinery	147685	111213	2667694	
	(5.54)	(4.17)	(100.00)	
Number of Units	72	29	1524	177846.27
Electrical machinery	26183	89495	765010	
	(3.42)	(11.70)	(100.00)	
Number of Units	46	22	488	5100.67
Miscellaneous	48201	0	414892	
manufacturing	(11.62)	(0.00)	(100.00)	
Number of Units	148	33	453	27659.47
Gas manufacturing	0	0	46658	
	(0.00)	(0.00)	(100.00)	
Number of Units	0	0	30	3100.53
Medical loans	85221	0	865883	
	(9.84)	(0.00)	(100.00)	
Number of Units	94	0	577	57725.53
Fishers loans	0	0	0	
	0	0	0	
Number of Units	0	0	28	0.0
Electricity generation supply	2563	34552	121435	
	(2.11)	(28.45)	(100.00)	
Number of Units	16	5	46	8095.67
Services	309988	145684	3134647	
	(9.89)	(4.65)	(100.00)	
Number of Units	688	76	4683	208976.47
Other industries	65004	1405136	7980145	
	(0.81)	(17.61)	(100.00)	
Number of Units	300	188	3007	532009
TOTAL	5721075	4347301	43187244	

Source: Various Annual Repots of APSFC

Note: The figures in parentheses indicates percentages to total.

to Rs. 145,684 lakhs (4.65%). Machinery Industry accounted for an average amount of Rs. 1778,46,3.27 lakhs with a total number of 1524 units.

However, the sanctions to the industry declined from Rs. 147,683 lakhs (5.54%) to Rs. 111,213 lakhs (4.17%) during the post-reform period. Non-metallic industry got an average sanction of Rs. 114,56,4.87 lakhs. The sanctions to non-metallic industry also decreased from Rs. 226,567 lakhs (13.16%) to Rs. 11,503 lakhs (0.67%) by 2005-06. In the case of Paper Products Industry the average amount stood at Rs. 114,56,4.87 lakhs covering 2326 units. It can be observed from the table that the Metal industry, petroleum products also claimed sanctions significantly during the same period.

However Fisheries Industry, Beverage and Tobacco, Gas Manufacturing Industry, Petroleum Products, Leather Products, Wood Products Industry, Electricity Generation Supply Industries have been getting lesser amounts of sanctions during the post reform period.

Industry-wise Disbursements During Post-Reform Period

The statistical information relating to the industry-wise disbursements of loans during the pre-reform period is given in Table 4.4. As can be seen from the table, the 'Other Industries' category is occupying first place claiming an average amount of Rs. 513,81,7.87 lakhs. The disbursements to this category increased from Rs. 80,402 lakhs to Rs. 1326,487 lakhs during the post-reform period in percentages terms, this forms 17.21 per cent in the total amount disbursed. The food industry secured second position with an average amount of Rs. 33,54,65.6 lakhs. The food industry is followed by Chemical Products Industry with an average amount of Rs. 249,287 lakhs. The disbursements to chemical products industry increased substantially from Rs. 14,275 lakhs in 1991-92 (0.38%) to Rs. 506,719 lakhs (13.55%) in 2005-06. The corporation has disbursed an average amount of Rs. 153,99,8.93

lakhs to Service Industry. The Non-Metallic Products obtained disbursements on an average amount of Rs. 145,26,6.47 lakhs. While Machinery Industry took an average amount of Rs. 134,26,7.47 lakhs. The average disbursements to Basic Metal Industry stood at Rs. 845,66.8 lakhs. While the Electrical Machinery, Metal Products got on an average of Rs. 58,70,0.13 lakhs Rs. 56,60,6.67 lakhs respectively.

However, Fisheries, Medical, Gas Manufacturing Industry, Petroleum Products, Leather Products, Wood Products Industries have secured fewer amounts of disbursements during the post reform period.

Table 4.4 : Industry-wise Disbursements in Post-Reform Period

(Amount in Rs. Lakhs)

Industry/Year	1991-92	2005-06	Total	AVG Amount
1	2	3	4	5
Food products	225097	504018	5031984	
	(4.47)	(10.06)	(100.00)	
Number of Units	713	131	3258	335465.6
Beverage& tobacco	1333	60601	459876	
	(0.29)	(13.18)	(100.00)	
Number of Units	1	15	174	30658.4
Textiles	126218	167174	2251958	
	(5.60)	(7.42)	(100.00)	
Number of Units	274	20	1842	150130.53
Wood products	13364	10848	149591	
	(8.93)	(7.25)	(100.00)	
Number of Units	144	20	433	9972.73
Paper& paper products	36059	124247	770933	
	(4.68)	(16.12)	(100.00)	
Number of Units	86	20	434	51395.35
Printing and publishing	37010	12679	535497	
	(6.91)	(2.37)	(100.00)	
Number of Units	117	5	386	35699.8

1	2	3	4	5
Leather products	27770	23494	147943	
	(18.77)	(15.88)	(100.00)	
Number of Units	107	7	172	9862.87
Rubber products	34270	0	302871	
	(11.32)	(0.00)	(100.00)	
Number of Units	71	0	294	20191.4
Chemical products	14275	506719	3739305	
	(0.38)	(13.55)	(100.00)	
Number of Units	150	99	1678	249287
Non-metallic products	158668	258262	2178997	
	(7.28)	(11.85)	(100.00)	
Number of Units	402	127	2328	145266.47
Transports vechiles &	8228	9412	299622	
spareparts	(2.75)	(3.14)	(100.00)	
Number of Units	14	4	106	19974.8
Petroleum products	5992	0	108132	
	(5.54)	(0.00)	(100.00)	
Number of Units	62	0	132	7208.8
Basic metal industry	44509	301744	1268502	
	(3.51)	(23.79)	(100.00)	
Number of Units	35	23	426	84566.8
Metal products	27033	54412	849100	
	(3.18)	(6.41)	(100.00)	
Number of Units	94	20	614	56606.67
Machinery	74944	110457	2014012	
	(3.72)	(5.48)	(100.00)	
Number of Units	72	29	1524	134267.47
Electrical machinery	17519	102482	880502	
	(1.99)	(11.64)	(100.00)	
Number of Units	46	22	488	58700.13
Miscellaneous	39502	100222	486196	
manufacturing	(8.15)	(20.63)	(100.00)	
Number of Units	148	33	453	32413.07

(Contd. ...)

1	2	3	4	5
Gas manufacturing	2912	0	59251	
	(4.91)	(0.00)	(100.00)	
Number of Units	148	33	453	3950.07
Medical loans	59254	0	677713	
	(8.74)	(0.00)	(100.00)	
Number of Units	94	0	577	45180.87
Fishers loans	0	0	0	
	0	0	0	
Number of Units	0	0	28	0
Electricity generation supply	1440	51216	201772	
	(0.71)	(25.38)	(100.00)	
Number of Units	16	5	46	13451.47
Services	278148	104706	2309984	
	(12.04)	(4.53)	(100.00)	
Number of Units	688	76	4683	153998.93
Other industries	80402	1326487	7707268	
	(1.04)	(17.21)	(100.00)	
Number of Units	300	188	3007	513817.87
TOTAL	1313947	3829180	32431009	

Source: Various Annual Repots of APSFC

Note: The figures in parentheses indicates percentages to total.

SECTION II
CONSTITUTION-WISE ASSISTANT GIVEN BY APSFC

The corporation extends financial assistance to all forms of organization starting from proprietory concerns to corporate bodies with various forms of organisations offering several kinds of advantages. The corporation does not distinguish between these forms organisations in different sectors in the matter of extensions of financial assistance. Here an attempt is made in this section to analyse the disbursements made by APSFC to various forms of organisation in the categories of Medium Scale Industries (MSIs) and Small Scale Industries (SSIs) during the study period.

Number of Units in MSI Assisted in APSFC During the Pre-Reform Period

The information relating to the constitution-wise number of units assisted by the APSFC, is shown in Table 4.5. It shows that number of units assisted by the corporation under various forms of organization, which included Public limited companies, Private limited companies, Co-operatives, Partnership concerns, Joint-Hindu Family concerns, proprietary concerns, and others. It is evident from the table that the total number of units during the pre-reform period is worked out to be highest in respect of proprietary concerns (73.17%) followed by partnership concerns (19.07%) and then the private limited companies (7.53%).

The analysis shown in Table 4.5 revealed that the proprietary concerns accounted for the highest percentage in the total number of units assisted by the APSFC through out the pre-reform period with the exception of the two years, i.e. 1979-80 and 1980-81. It is interesting to note that the number of Joint Hindu Family concerns is the lowest percentage of units to be assisted by APSFC in all the years of pre-reform period.

Number of Units in MSI Assisted in APSFC During the Post-Reform Period

The data relating to number of units assisted by the APSFC in the forms of disbursements during the post reform period is shown in Table 4.6. It is evident from the table that the total number of units assisted during the post reform period is found to be highest in respect of proprietary concerns (46.72%) followed by partnership concerns (35.35%) and private limited companies (13.05%).

The year-wise analysis also revealed that the number of proprietary concerns accounted for the highest percentage in the total number of units assisted by the APSFC with the highest percentage in the total number of units assisted by

Table 4.5 : Number of Units Assisted by APSFC during the Pre-Reform Period to MSIs

Year	Pub Lit Pub Pvt. Ltd.	Private Ltd. Co.	Co-operatives	Partnership concerns	Joint Hindu families	Proprietary concerns	Others	Total
1	2	3	4	5	6	7	8	9
1976-77	22	18	4	122	1	250	0	417
	(5.28)	(4.32)	(0.96)	(29.26)	(0.24)	(59.95)	(0.00)	(100.00)
1977-78	8	41	10	165	2	420	0	646
	(1.24)	(6.35)	(1.55)	(25.54)	(0.31)	(65.02)	(0.00)	(100.00)
1978-79	10	71	4	151	0	477	0	713
	(1.40)	(9.96)	(0.56)	(21.18)	(0.00)	(66.90)	(0.00)	(100.00)
1979-80	15	27	0	400	0	376	0	818
	(1.83)	(3.30)	(0.00)	(48.90)	(0.00)	(45.97)	(0.00)	(100.00)
1980-81	24	83	6	595	0	351	0	1059
	(2.27)	(7.84)	(0.57)	(56.19)	(0.00)	(33.14)	(0.00)	(100.00)
1981-82	16	98	0	402	0	6269	0	6785
	(0.24)	(1.44)	(0.00)	(5.92)	(0.00)	(92.39)	(0.00)	(100.00)
1982-83	18	94	0	370	1	934	3	1420
	(1.27)	(6.62)	(0.00)	(26.06)	(0.07)	(65.77)	(0.21)	(100.00)
1983-84	17	105	2	502	0	2004	0	2630
	(0.65)	(3.99)	(0.08)	(19.09)	(0.00)	(76.20)	(0.00)	(100.00)

1984-85	15	131	1	450	0	854	1	1452
	(1.03)	(9.02)	(0.07)	(30.99)	(0.00)	(58.82)	(0.07)	(100.00)
1985-86	9	137	0	599	0	814	0	1559
	(0.58)	(8.79)	(0.00)	(38.42)	(0.00)	(52.21)	(0.00)	(100.00)
1986-87	11	174	0	447	1	873	0	1506
	0.73)	(11.55)	(0.00)	(29.68)	(0.07)	(57.97)	(0.00)	(100.00)
1987-88	15	233	2	383	0	971	0	1604
	(0.94)	(14.53)	(0.12)	(23.88)	(0.00)	(60.54)	(0.00)	(100.00)
1988-89	40	246	1	439	0	1646	1	2373
	(1.69)	(10.37)	(0.04)	(18.50)	(0.00)	(69.36)	(0.04)	(100.00)
1989-90	41	452	0	478	0	2617	2	3590
	(1.14)	(12.59)	(0.00)	(13.31)	(0.00)	(72.90)	(0.06)	(100.00)
1990-91	36	487	0	565	0	4422	0	5510
	(0.65)	(8.84)	(0.00)	(10.25)	(0.00)	(80.25)	(0.00)	(100.00)
Constitution-wise	296	2397	30	6068	05	23278	07	31814
Total	(0.93)	(7.53)	(0.09)	(19.07)	(0.05)	(73.17)	(0.2)	(100.00)

Source: Various Annual Repots of APSFC

Note: The figures in parentheses indicates percentages to total.

Table 4.6 : Number of Units Assisted by APSFC during the Post-Reform Period to MSIs

Year	Pub Lit. Pub Pvt. Ltd.	Private Ltd. Co.	Co-opera-tives	Partner-ship concerns	Joint Hindu families	Proprietary concerns	Others	Total
1	2	3	4	5	6	7	8	9
1991-92	14	59	0	36	0	73	0	182
	(7.69)	(32.42)	(0.00)	(19.78)	(0.00)	(40.11)	(0.00)	(100.00)
1992-93	8	25	0	24	0	74	2	133
	(6.02)	(18.80)	(0.00)	(18.05)	(0.00)	(55.64)	(1.50)	(100.00)
1993-94	6	20	0	44	0	42	0	112
	(5.36)	(17.86)	(0.00)	(39.29)	(0.00)	(37.50)	(0.00)	(100.00)
1994-95	7	66	0	34	0	97	1	205
	(3.41)	(32.20)	(0.00)	(16.59)	(0.00)	(47.32)	(0.49)	(100.00)
1995-96	10	23	0	22	0	84	5	144
	(6.94)	(15.97)	(0.00)	(15.28)	(0.00)	(58.33)	(3.47)	(100.00)
1996-97	9	28	0	30	0	44	0	111
	(8.11)	(25.23)	(0.00)	(27.03)	(0.00)	(39.64)	(0.00)	(100.00)
1997-98	12	28	0	40	0	61	0	141
	(8.51)	(19.86)	(0.00)	(28.37)	(0.00)	(43.26)	(0.00)	(100.00)
1998-99	10	31	0	57	0	82	1	181
	(5.52)	(17.13)	(0.00)	(31.49)	(0.00)	(45.30)	(0.55)	(100.00)

1999-00	13	32	0	44	0	105	0	194
	(6.70)	(16.49)	(0.00)	(22.68)	(0.00)	(54.12)	(0.00)	(100.00)
2001-01	0	0	0	0	0	0	0	0
	(0.00)	(0.00)	(0.00)	(0.00)	(0.00)	(0.00)	(0.00)	(0.00)
2001-02	20	90	0	907	0	302	2	1321
	(1.51)	(6.81)	(0.00)	(68.66)	(0.00)	(22.86)	(0.15)	(100.00)
2002-03	13	37	1	50	0	239	1	341
	(3.81)	(10.85)	(0.29)	(14.66)	(0.00)	(70.09)	(0.29)	(100.00)
2003-04	28	37	0	59	0	233	1	358
	(7.82)	(10.34)	(0.00)	(16.48)	(0.00)	(65.08)	(0.28)	(100.00)
2004-05	17	31	2	54	0	231	0	335
	(5.07)	(9.25)	(0.60)	(16.12)	(0.00)	(68.96)	(0.00)	(100.00)
2005-06	14	31	0	56	0	259	4	364
	(3.85)	(8.52)	(0.00)	(15.38)	(0.00)	(71.15)	(1.10)	(100.00)
Constitution-wise	181	538	03	1457	0	1926	17	4122
Total	(11.39)	(13.05)	(0.01)	(35.35)	(0.00)	(46.72)	(0.41)	(100.00)

Source: Various Annual Repots of APSFC

Note: The figures in parentheses indicates percentages to total.

the APSFC with the exception of two years viz., 1993-94 and 2001-2002. It is interesting to note that the joint Hindu families is the lowest percentage units be assisted by APSFC. Thus, it may be inferred from the analysis that during both pre-reform period and post- reform period, propriety concerns accounted for more number of units assisted by APSFC. While joint Hindu families concerns accounted for less number of units assisted by the APSFC.

Disbursements to MSIs During Pre-Reform Period

The data relating to amounts disbursed by the Corporation during the pre-reform period to Medium Scale Industries (MSIs) are given in Table 4.7. It is evident from the table that private limited companies received the highest share (39.48%) in the amount of total disbursements by the Corporation during the pre-reform period. The share of proprietary concerns is 27.10%, followed by the partnership concerns (26.32%) with regard to in the amount of total disbursements made by APSFC. But Joint Hindu family concerns, co-operatives, could not claim much amount of disbursements out of the total disbursements.

Amount Disbursed by APSFC During Post-Reform Period

The amount disbursed by the APSFC during the post-reform period to MSIs given in Table 4.8. It is interesting to note that public limited companies have claimed (45.42%) of the total disbursements made by APSFC. Followed by private limited companies (22.22%), proprietary concerns (18.39%), partnership concerns (13.70%). However the Joint Hindu Families did not receive any amount by way of disbursements from the APSFC.

Number of Units Disbursed by APSFC to SSIs During the Pre-Reform Period

The data relating to the number of units disbursed by APSFC are shown in Table 4.9. It can be observed from the table that proprietary concerns accounted for the highest percentage 73.72 of the total number of units disbursed by APSFC followed by Partnership Concerns (18.94%), Private Limited Companies accounted 6.97 percent, during the total pre-reform period. The year-wise analysis also reveled that proprietary concerns accounted for the highest percentage in the total number of units assisted by APSFC with the exception of the year 1978-79.

Number of Units Disbursed by APSFC to SSIs During the Post-Reform Period

The data relating to the number of units disbursed by APSFC during the post-reform period to SSIs are shown in Table 4.10. It is observed from the table proprietary concerns claimed the largest share with 68.74%, followed by partnership concerns (20.74%), private limited companies (9.56%), public limited companies (0.74%), and others (0.11%) in the total post-reform period. But the joint Hindu families concerns could not figure in the number of units disbursed during the post-reform period. The year-wise analysis also revealed that the proprietary concerns accounted for highest number of units disbursed, while the Joint families concerns could not registered for disbursements.

Amount Disbursed by APSFC to SSIs During the Pre-Reform Period

The data relating to the amount disbursed by APSFC during the pre-reform period are shown in Table 4.11. It can be observed from the table that proprietary concerns received an amount of Rs. 2,66,40 crores claiming 38.32 per cent of the total disbursements made by the APSFC during pre-reform

Table 4.7 : Number of Units Assisted by APSFC during the Pre-Reform Period to MSIs

Year	Pub Lit Pub Pvt. Ltd.	Private Ltd. Co.	Co-operatives	Partnership concerns	Joint Hindu families	Proprietary concerns	Others	Total
1	2	3	4	5	6	7	8	9
1976-77	124	233	16	214	0	148	0	736
	(16.88)	(31.66)	(2.18)	(29.10)	(0.03)	(20.15)	(0.00)	(100.00)
1977-78	188	453	3	218	0	128	14	1004
	(18.72)	(45.09)	(0.34)	(21.71)	(0.00)	(12.74)	(1.41)	(100.00)
1978-79	221	468	0	700	0	217	0	1606
	(13.77)	(29.15)	(0.00)	(43.55)	(0.00)	(13.53)	(0.00)	(100.00)
1979-80	346	723	34	1066	0	418	0	2588
	(13.37)	(27.95)	(1.33)	(41.20)	(0.00)	(16.14)	(0.02)	(100.00)
1980-81	314	999	3	936	0	733	14	2999
	(10.48)	(33.30)	(0.11)	(31.19)	(0.00)	(24.45)	(0.48)	(100.00)
1981-82	334	986	25	1084	1	1328	41	3799
	(8.78)	(25.96)	(0.66)	(28.54)	(0.02)	(34.96)	(1.07)	(100.00)
1982-83	363	1275	1	1387	0	1417	0	4443
	(8.17)	(28.69)	(0.02)	(31.23)	(0.00)	(31.89)	(0.00)	(100.00)
1983-84	362	1358	3	5412	0	2365	1	9501
	(4.00)	(14.0)	(0.00)	(57.00)	(0.00)	(25.00)	(0.00)	(100.00)

1984-85	258	2000	0	2399	0	1197	0	5854
	(4.00)	(34.0)	(0.00)	(41.00)	(0.00)	(20.00)	(0.00)	(100.00)
1985-86	409	2881	8	1914	3	1446	100	6762
	(6.00)	(43.0)	(0.00)	(28.00)	(0.00)	(21.00)	(1.00)	(100.00)
1986-87	363	4408	7	1631	0	1445	55	7909
	(5.00)	(56.0)	(0.00)	(21.00)	(0.00)	(18.00)	(1.00)	(100.00)
1987-88	926	4848	6	1722	0	2402	4	9908
	(9.00)	(49.0)	(0.00)	(17.00)	(0.00)	(24.00)	(0.00)	(100.00)
1988-89	945	5377	3	1842	0	2839	7	11012
	(9.00)	(49.0)	(0.00)	(17.00)	(0.00)	(26.00)	(0.00)	(100.00)
1989-90	770	5619	4	2010	0	4026	0	12429
	(6.00)	(45.0)	(0.00)	(16.00)	(0.00)	(32.00)	(0.00)	(100.00)
1990-91	422	5694	4	2346	0	5507	2	13975
	(3.00)	(41.0)	(0.00)	(17.00)	(0.00)	(39.00)	(0.00)	(100.00)
Constitution Wise	6345	37322	117	24881	4	25616	238	94523
Total	(6.71)	(39.48)	(0.12)	(26.32)	(0.00)	(27.10)	(0.25)	(100.00)

Source: Various Annual Repots of APSFC

Note: The figures in parentheses indicates percentages to total.

Table 4.8 : Amount Disbursed by APSFC to MSIs During the Post-Reform Period

Year	Pub Lit Pub Pvt. Ltd.	Private Ltd. Co.	Co-operatives	Partnership concerns	Joint Hindu families	Proprietary concerns	Others	Total
1	2	3	4	5	6	7	8	9
1991-92	49453	159752	0	34159	0	27716	0	271080
	(18.24)	(58.93)	(0.00)	(12.60)	(0.00)	(10.22)	(0.00)	(100.00)
1992-93	35025	244176	0	39133	0	42101	1501	361936
	(9.68)	(67.46)	(0.00)	(10.81)	(0.00)	(11.63)	(0.41)	(100.00)
1993-94	14370	69001	0	28150	0	25256	0	136777
	(10.51)	(50.45)	(0.00)	(20.58)	(0.00)	(18.47)	(0.00)	(100.00)
1994-95	20851	142928	0	25197	0	66602	802	256380
	(8.13)	(55.75)	(0.00)	(9.83)	(0.00)	(25.98)	(0.31)	(100.00)
1995-96	55844	156175	0	63743	0	40910	6514	323186
	(17.28)	(48.32)	(0.00)	(19.72)	(0.00)	(12.66)	(2.02)	(100.00)
1996-97	60721	110560	0	54277	0	43353	0	268911
	(22.58)	(41.11)	(0.00)	(20.18)	(0.00)	(16.12)	(0.00)	(100.00)
1997-98	47802	118172	0	55910	0	93120	0	315004
	(15.18)	(37.51)	(0.00)	(17.75)	(0.00)	(29.56)	(0.00)	(100.00)
1998-99	73553	147646	0	93518	0	83621	179	398517
	(18.46)	(37.05)	(0.00)	(23.47)	(0.00)	(20.98)	(0.04)	(100.00)

1999-00	89555	233416	0	87548	0	133722	0	544241
	(16.46)	(42.89)	(0.00)	(16.09)	(0.00)	(24.57)	(0.00)	(100.00)
2001-01	0	0	0	0	0	0	0	0
	(0.00)	(0.00)	(0.00)	(0.00)	(0.00)	(0.00)	(0.00)	(0.00)
2001-02	48750	150000	0	482391	0	450883	4763	1136787
	(4.29)	(13.20)	(0.00)	(42.43)	(0.00)	(39.66)	(0.42)	(100.00)
2002-03	228629	347061	13050	183875	0	377044	1500	1151159
	(19.86)	(30.15)	(1.13)	(15.97)	(0.00)	(32.75)	(0.13)	(100.00)
2003-04	236222	309521	0	205424	0	377044	1500	1129711
	(20.91)	(27.40)	(0.00)	(18.18)	(0.00)	(33.38)	(0.13)	(100.00)
2004-05	333953	485787	4942	196332	0	445287	0	1466301
	(22.78)	(33.13)	(0.34)	(13.39)	(0.00)	(30.37)	(0.00)	(100.00)
2005-06	539808	600189	0	469235	0	503656	4555	2117443
	(25.49)	(28.34)	(0.00)	(22.16)	(0.00)	(23.79)	(0.22)	(100.00)
Constitution-wise	6692812	3274384	17992	2018892	0	2710315	21314	14735713
Total	(45.42)	(22.22)	(0.12)	(13.70)	(0.00)	(18.39)	(0.14)	(100.00)

Source: Various Annual Repots of APSFC

Note: The figures in parentheses indicates percentages to total.

Table 4.9 : Number of Units Assisted by APSFC During The Pre-Reform Period to MSI's

Year	Pub Lit Pub Pvt. Ltd.	Private Ltd. Co.	Co-operatives	Partnership concerns	Joint Hindu families	Proprietary concerns	Others	Total
1	2	3	4	5	6	7	8	9
1976-77	3	28	9	163	0	420	6	629
	(0.48)	(4.45)	(1.43)	(25.91)	(0.00)	(66.77)	(0.95)	(100.00)
1977-78	2	53	4	150	0	477	0	686
	(0.29)	(7.73)	(0.58)	(21.87)	(0.00)	(69.53)	(0.00)	(100.00)
1978-79	4	55	6	396	0	375	0	836
	(0.48)	(6.58)	(0.72)	(47.37)	(0.00)	(44.86)	(0.00)	(100.00)
1979-80	6	51	0	589	0	649	0	1295
	(0.46)	(3.94)	(0.00)	(45.48)	(0.00)	(50.12)	(0.00)	(100.00)
1980-81	2	57	0	386	0	6265	0	6710
	(0.03)	(0.85)	(0.00)	(5.75)	(0.00)	(93.37)	(0.00)	(100.00)
1981-82	1	59	0	361	1	939	0	1361
	(0.07)	(4.34)	(0.00)	(26.52)	(0.07)	(68.99)	(0.00)	(100.00)
1982-83	2	73	2	502	0	2002	0	2581
	(0.08)	(2.83)	(0.08)	(19.45)	(0.00)	(77.57)	(0.00)	(100.00)
1983-84	5	111	1	450	0	833	0	1400
	(0.36)	(7.93)	(0.07)	(32.14)	(0.00)	(59.50)	(0.00)	(100.00)

1984-85	2	99	0	557	0	813	1	1472
	(0.14)	(6.73)	(0.00)	(37.84)	(0.00)	(55.23)	(0.07)	(100.00)
1985-86	4	121	0	446	1	873	0	1445
	(0.28)	(8.37)	(0.00)	(30.87)	(0.07)	(60.42)	(0.00)	(100.00)
1986-87	5	163	2	381	0	971	0	1522
	(0.33)	(10.71)	(0.13)	(25.03)	(0.00)	(63.80)	(0.00)	(100.00)
1987-88	17	204	1	429	0	1642	1	2294
	(0.74)	(8.89)	(0.04)	(18.70)	(0.00)	(71.58)	(0.04)	(100.00)
1988-89	21	351	0	436	0	1686	2	2496
	(0.84)	(14.06)	(0.00)	(17.47)	(0.00)	(67.55)	(0.08)	(100.00)
1989-90	12	403	0	536	0	2076	0	3027
	(0.40)	(13.31)	(0.00)	(17.71)	(0.00)	(68.58)	(0.00)	(100.00)
1990-91	3	552	1	684	0	5144	0	6384
	(0.05)	(8.65)	(0.02)	(10.71)	(0.00)	(80.58)	(0.00)	(100.00)
Constitution-wise	89	2380	26	6466	2	25165	10	34138
Total	(0.26)	(6.97)	(0.08)	(18.94)	(0.00)	(73.72)	(0.03)	(100.00)

Source: Various Annual Repots of APSFC
Note: The figures in parentheses indicates percentages to total.

Table 4.10 : Number of Units Assisted by APSFC During The Pre-Reform Period to MSI's

Year	Pub Lit Pub Pvt. Ltd.	Private Ltd. Co.	Co-operatives	Partnership concerns	Joint Hindu families	Proprietary concerns	Others	Total
1	2	3	4	5	6	7	8	9
1991-92	11	272	1	543	0	4047	0	4874
	(0.23)	(5.58)	(0.02)	(11.14)	(0.00)	(83.03)	(0.00)	(100.00)
1992-93	2	93	2	344	0	1777	4	2222
	(0.09)	(4.19)	(0.09)	(15.48)	(0.00)	(79.97)	(0.18)	(100.00)
1993-94	5	128	3	215	0	1209	0	1560
	(0.32)	(8.21)	(0.19)	(13.78)	(0.00)	(77.50)	(0.00)	(100.00)
1994-95	4	124	2	154	0	602	4	890
	(0.45)	(13.93)	(0.22)	(17.30)	(0.00)	(67.64)	(0.45)	(100.00)
1995-96	8	155	1	224	0	484	2	874
	(0.92)	(17.73)	(0.11)	(25.63)	(0.00)	(55.38)	(0.23)	(100.00)
1996-97	7	98	1	213	0	748	0	1067
	(0.66)	(9.18)	(0.09)	(19.96)	(0.00)	(70.10)	(0.00)	(100.00)
1997-98	13	113	2	274	0	493	0	895
	(1.45)	(12.63)	(0.22)	(30.61)	(0.00)	(55.08)	(0.00)	(100.00)
1998-99	15	113	1	294	0	492	5	920
	(1.63)	(12.28)	(0.11)	(31.96)	(0.00)	(53.48)	(0.54)	(100.00)

1999-00	17	155	1	345	0	815	1	1334
	(1.27)	(11.62)	(0.07)	(25.86)	(0.00)	(61.09)	(0.07)	(100.00)
2001-01	0	0	0	0	0	0	0	0
	(0.00)	(0.00)	(0.00)	(0.00)	(0.00)	(0.00)	(0.00)	(100.00)
2001-02	12	0	0	410	0	600	4	1026
	(1.17)	(0.00)	(0.00)	(39.96)	(0.00)	(58.48)	(0.39)	(100.00)
2002-03	16	142	0	222	0	446	0	826
	(1.94)	(17.19)	(0.00)	(26.88)	(0.00)	(54.00)	(0.00)	(100.00)
2003-04	13	140	3	223	0	329	0	708
	(1.84)	(19.77)	(0.42)	(31.50)	(0.00)	(46.47)	(0.00)	(100.00)
2004-05	9	121	0	208	0	404	0	742
	(1.21)	(16.31)	(0.00)	(28.03)	(0.00)	(54.45)	(0.00)	(100.00)
2005-06	6	117	2	174	0	292	1	592
	(1.01)	(19.76)	(0.34)	(29.39)	(0.00)	(49.32)	(0.17)	(100.00)
Constitution-wise	138	1771	19	3843	0	12738	21	18530
Total	(0.74)	(9.56)	(0.10)	(20.74)	(0.00)	(68.74)	(0.11)	(100.00)

Source: Various Annual Repots of APSFC

Note: The figures in parentheses indicates percentages to total.

Table 4.11 : Number of Units Assisted by APSFC During The Pre-Reform Period to MSI's

Year	Pub Lit Pub Pvt. Ltd.	Private Ltd. Co.	Co-operatives	Partnership concerns	Joint Hindu families	Proprietary concerns	Others	Total
1	2	3	4	5	6	7	8	9
1976-77	4	125	6	201	0	148	8	492
	(1.00)	(25.00)	(1.00)	(41.00)	(0.00)	(30.00)	(2.00)	(100.00)
1977-78	14	245	3	213	0	128	0	604
	(2.00)	(41.00)	(1.00)	(35.00)	(0.00)	(21.00)	(0.00)	(100.00)
1978-79	16	214	0	677	0	213	0	1120
	(1.00)	(19.00)	(0.00)	(60.00)	(0.00)	(19.00)	(0.00)	(100.00)
1979-80	18	280	34	991	0	409	0	1732
	(1.00)	(16.00)	(2.00)	(57.00)	(0.00)	(24.00)	(0.00)	(100.00)
1980-81	13	302	0	828	0	711	0	1855
	(1.00)	(16.00)	(0.00)	(45.00)	(0.00)	(38.00)	(0.00)	(100.00)
1981-82	7	461	0	949	3	1324	0	2745
	(0.00)	(17.00)	(0.00)	(35.00)	(0.00)	(48.00)	(0.00)	(100.00)
1982-83	67	592	1	387	0	1443	0	2490
	(3.00)	(24.00)	(0.00)	(16.00)	(0.00)	(58.00)	(0.00)	(100.00)
1983-84	25	667	3	3082	0	0	0	3 7 7 8
	(1.00)	(18.00)	(0.00)	(82.00)	(0.00)	(0.00)	(0.00)	(100.00)

1984-85	70	1138	0	2392	0	1194	55	4848
	(1.00)	(23.00)	(0.00)	(49.00)	(0.00)	(25.00)	(1.00)	(100.00)
1985-86	48	1622	0	1897	3	1445	0	5015
	(1.00)	(32.00)	(0.00)	(38.00)	(0.00)	(29.00)	(0.00)	(100.00)
1986-87	23	2340	8	1573	0	1445	0	5389
	(0.00)	(43.00)	(0.00)	(29.00)	(0.00)	(27.00)	(0.00)	(100.00)
1987-88	175	3149	7	1375	0	2359	4	7070
	2.00)	(45.00)	(0.00)	(19.00)	(0.00)	(33.00)	(0.00)	(100.00)
1988-89	219	3407	0	1592	0	2751	7	7976
	(3.00)	(43.00)	(0.00)	(20.00)	(0.00)	(34.00)	(0.00)	(100.00)
1989-90	161	3801	0	1731	0	3793	0	9486
	(2.00)	(40.00)	(0.00)	(18.00)	(0.00)	(40.00)	(0.00)	(100.00)
1990-91	59	4267	3	2113	0	5277	0	11719
	(1.00)	(36.00)	(0.00)	(18.00)	(0.00)	(45.00)	(0.00)	(100.00)
Constitution-wise	59	22610	65	20066	6	26640	77	69523
Total	(0.08)	(32.52)	(0.09)	(28.86)	(0.01)	(38.32)	(0.11)	(100.00)

Source: Various Annual Repots of APSFC

Note: The figures in parentheses indicates percentages to total.

Table 4.12 : Number of Units Assisted by APSFC During The Pre-Reform Period to MSI's

Year	Pub Lit Pub Pvt. Ltd.	Private Ltd. Co.	Co-operatives	Partnership concerns	Joint Hindu families	Proprietary concerns	Others	Total
1	2	3	4	5	6	7	8	9
1991-92	104410	364013	258	276014	0	567902	6	1312603
	(7.95)	(27.73)	(0.02)	(21.03)	(0.00)	(43.27)	(0.00)	(100.00)
1992-93	3980	338399	399	2496060	0	306419	1070	3146327
	(0.13)	(10.76)	(0.01)	(79.33)	(0.00)	(9.74)	(0.03)	(100.00)
1993-94	11176	298033	1188	165087	204	216998	0	692686
	(1.61)	(43.03)	(0.17)	(23.83)	(0.03)	(31.33)	(0.00)	(100.00)
1994-95	10047	303139	941	108987	0	183677	897	607688
	(1.65)	(49.88)	(0.15)	(17.93)	(0.00)	(30.23)	(0.15)	(100.00)
1995-96	37283	369971	774	191674	0	236061	1885	837648
	(4.45)	(44.17)	(0.09)	(22.88)	(0.00)	(28.18)	(0.23)	(100.00)
1996-97	28486	293591	596	227477	0	302419	0	852569
	(3.34)	(34.44)	(0.07)	(26.68)	(0.00)	(35.47)	(0.00)	(100.00)
1997-98	41809	300691	2507	327630	0	323663	0	996300
	(4.20)	(30.18)	(0.25)	(32.88)	(0.00)	(32.49)	(0.00)	(100.00)
1998-99	67250	383389	1296	400975	0	365150	4458	1222518
	(5.50)	(31.36)	(0.11)	(32.80)	(0.00)	(29.87)	(0.36)	(100.00)

1999-00	87441 (4.17)	675153 (32.19)	1900 (0.09)	666808 (31.79)	0 (0.00)	661558 (31.54)	4661 (0.22)	2097521 (100.00)
2001-01	0 (0.00)	0 (0.00)	0 (0.00)	0 (0.00)	0 (0.00)	0 (0.00)	0 (0.00)	0 (0.00)
2001-02	9740 (0.74)	0 (0.00)	0 (0.00)	507603 (38.62)	0 (0.00)	742110 (56.46)	55000 (4.18)	1314453 (100.00)
2002-03	100642 (5.53)	728463 (40.04)	3407 (0.19)	452269 (24.86)	0 (0.00)	534408 (29.38)	0 (0.00)	1819189 (100.00)
2003-04	96908 (5.69)	599009 (35.20)	4480 (0.26)	512288 (30.10)	0 (0.00)	489152 (28.74)	0 (0.00)	1701837 (100.00)
2004-05	86383 (4.28)	850409 (42.13)	0 (0.00)	459833 (22.78)	0 (0.00)	622035 (30.81)	0 (0.00)	2018660 (100.00)
2005-06	96989 (4.62)	996795 (47.52)	4488 (0.21)	548085 (26.13)	0 (0.00)	451284 (21.51)	110 (0.01)	2097751 (100.00)
Constitution-wise Total	782544 (3.7)	6501055 (31.38)	22234 (0.11)	7340790 (35.43)	204 (0.00)	6002836 (28.97)	68087 (0.33)	20717750 (100.00)

Source: Various Annual Repots of APSFC

Note: The figures in parentheses indicates percentages to total.

period. Proprietary concerns is followed by Private Limited Companies with a share of 32.52 per cent, and partnership concerns with 28.86 per cent the year-wise analysis also indicates the similar picture.

Amount Disbursed by APSFC to SSIs During the Post-Reform Period

The data relating to the amount disbursed by APSFC during the post-reform period to SSIs are shown in Table 4.12. It is clear from the table that partnership concerns received an amount of Rs. 734,07,90 crores (35.43%). The next place goes to private limited companies which claimed an amount of Rs. 650,10,55 crores (31.38%). It is followed by proprietary concerns with Rs. 600,28,36 crores (28.97%). The public limited companies received an amount of Rs. 78,25,44 crores (3.7%). The co-operatives received lesser amount of disbursements (0.11%). While Joint Hindu families concerns did not figure.

SECTION III
APSFC'S CONTRIBUTION TO SSIs AND MSIs

One of the main objectives of APSFC is to strengthen the SSIs and MSIs in the State. In view of this, it is proposed to make an in-depth analysis of the financial contributions of APSFC to SS and MS industries in terms number of units, sanctions and disbursements during the pre- and post-reform period.

Number of SSI Units and MSI Units Sanctioned During Pre-Reform Period

The data relating to the number of units sanctioned by the corporation under to SSIs and MSIs category during the pre-reform period 1976-77 to 1990- 91 is presented in Table 4.13. It is heartening to note that a total number of 40407 units received sanctions from APSFC in 1976-77. Further, it is also interesting to observe that the number of units registered in 1976-77 were only 988 units where as the number

Table 4.13 : Number of Units Sanctioned During Pre Reform Period to SSIs and MSIs

Year	SSI	%to total	MSI	% to total	Total Units	Total(%)
1976-77	988	96.58	35	3.42	1023	100.00
1977-78	4589	92.56	369	7.44	4958	100.00
1978-79	1419	95.94	60	4.06	1479	100.00
1979-80	2060	97.31	57	2.69	2117	100.00
1980-81	2312	95.66	105	4.34	2417	100.00
1981-82	1796	96.15	72	3.85	1868	100.00
1982-83	3057	97.64	74	2.36	3131	100.00
1983-84	1819	96.91	58	3.09	1877	100.00
1984-85	1750	95.26	87	4.74	1837	100.00
1985-86	2111	95.95	89	4.05	2200	100.00
1986-87	2466	94.96	131	5.04	2597	100.00
1987-88	1032	88.13	139	11.87	1171	100.00
1988-89	3392	94.46	199	5.54	3591	100.00
1989-90	2419	92.86	186	7.14	2605	100.00
1990-91	9197	97.97	191	2.03	9388	100.00
Total	**40407**	**95.62**	**1852**	**4.38**	**42259**	**100.00**

Source: Various Annual Repots of APSFC

The figures in parentheses indicates percentages to total

of units registered in the year 1990-91 increased to 9171. From Table 4.13 it is also clear that the MSI units have given comparatively less priority in terms of assistance by the Corporation. The Corporation has sanctioned a total number of 1852 MSI units during pre-reform period and this constitutes 4.38 percent. On the other hand, the total number of units sanctioned under SSI category accounted for 95.62 percent during the pre reform period. From this it may be inferred that SSI units have been given preferential treatment over the MSI units during the pre-reform period.

Number of SSI Units and MSI Units Sanctioned During Post-Reform Period

The data pertaining to the post-reform period assistance extended by APSFC during the post-reform period are shown in Table 4.14.

Table 4.14 : Number of units sanctioned during post reform period to SSIs and MSIs

Year	SSI	%to total	MSI	% to total	Total Units	Total(%)
1991-92	4467	95.06	232	4.94	4699	100.00
1992-93	3144	92.77	245	7.23	3389	100.00
1993-94	1333	91.99	116	8.01	1449	100.00
1994-95	1077	89.30	129	10.70	1206	100.00
1995-96	1187	90.13	130	9.87	1317	100.00
1996-97	1032	88.97	128	11.03	1160	100.00
1997-98	1095	86.22	175	13.78	1270	100.00
1998-99	1090	86.17	175	13.83	1265	100.00
1999-00	1541	89.02	190	10.98	1731	100.00
2000-01	1450	84.11	274	15.89	1724	100.00
2001-02	1549	82.26	334	17.74	1883	100.00
2002-03	883	70.87	363	29.13	1246	100.00
2003-04	785	68.08	368	31.92	1153	100.00
2004-05	729	68.71	332	31.29	1061	100.00
2005-06	640	61.36	403	38.64	1043	100.00
Total	**22002**	**(85.95)**	**3594**	**(14.05)**	**25596**	**100.00**

Source: Various Annual Repots of APSFC

It reveals the number of units sanctioned during post-reform period. It is disheartening to note that the number of assisted SSI units declined from 4467 in 1991-92 to at 640 units in 2005-06. The total sanctioned to SSI units are 22,002 during the post-reform period. The table also provides information about MSIs. It is interesting to note that the MSIs number is 232 units in 1991-92 this number is registered to be 403 in 2005-

06. The total number of units sanctioned to MSI units are 3594. Out of the total number of 25,596 units sanctioned to both SSI and MSI units. The SSI accounted for 85.95 per cent and the MSIs accounted for 14.05 per cent.

Amounts of Sanctions and Disbursements made to SSIs and MSIs in the Pre-Reform Period

The Statistical information relating to the amounts sanctioned and disbursed to SSIs and MSIs is shown is Table 4.15.

Table 4.15 : APSFC Assistance to SSIs & MSI Units During Pre-Reform Period

(Amount in Rs. 000)

	SANCTIONS			DIBURSEMENTS		
Year	SSIs	MSI*	Total	SSIs	MSI	Total
1	2	3	4	5	6	7
1976-77	93841	55661	149502	48436	25163	73599
	(62.77)	(37.23)	(100.00)	(65.81)	(34.19)	(100.00)
1977-78	425164	382786	807950	36280	21762	58042
	(52.62)	(47.38)	(100.00)	(62.51)	(37.49)	(100.00)
1978-79	198156	95958	294114	112129	48504	160633
	(67.37)	(32.63)	(100.00)	(69.80)	(30.20)	(100.00)
1979-80	279593	94272	373865	173151	84980	258131
	(74.78)	(25.22)	(100.00)	(67.08)	(32.92)	(100.00)
1980-81	283185	183579	466764	184367	111717	296084
	(60.67)	(39.33)	(100.00)	(62.27)	(37.73)	(100.00)
1981-82	457882	158065	615947	272558	99032	371590
	(74.34)	(25.66)	(100.00)	(73.35)	(26.650	(100.00)
1982-83	515962	180487	696449	348997	100652	449649
	(74.08)	(25.92)	(100.00)	(77.62)	(22.380	(100.00)
1983-84	574765	156107	730872	377893	95305	473198
	(78.64)	(21.36)	(100.00)	(79.86)	(20.14)	(100.00)
1984-85	659690	233890	893580	479463	106018	585481
	(73.83)	(26.17)	(100.00)	(81.89)	(18.11)	(100.00)

1	2	3	4	5	6	7
1985-86	790763	273124	1063887	492461	163758	656219
	(74.33)	(25.67)	(100.00)	(75.05)	(24.95)	(100.00)
1986-87	848548	476603	1325151	544409	243889	788298
	(64.03)	(35.97)	(100.00)	(69.06)	(30.94)	(100.00)
1987-88	821025	452191	1273216	726953	263930	990883
	(64.48)	(35.52)	(100.00)	(73.36)	(26.64)	(100.00)
1988-89	1193741	444023	1637764	798183	303408	1101591
	(72.89)	(27.11)	(100.00)	(72.46)	(27.54)	(100.00)
1989-90	1470169	380131	1850300	948895	294063	1242958
	(79.46)	(20.54)	(100.00)	(76.34)	(23.66)	(100.00)
1990-91	19272288	538546	19810834.	1172183	225319	1397502
	(97.28)	(2.72)	(100.00)	(83.88)	(16.12)	(100.00)
Total	27884772	4105423	31990195	6716358	2817500	8903858
	(87.17)	(12.83)	(100.00)	(70.45)	(29.55)	(100.00)
Exponential	22.4*	12.1*		22.2*	17.2*	
Growth	t-(5.709)	t-(4.598)		t-(11.719)	t-(8.819)	

*Significant at 1 per cent level.
Source: Annual Reports of APSFC.
Note: The figures in parentheses in indicate percentages to total.

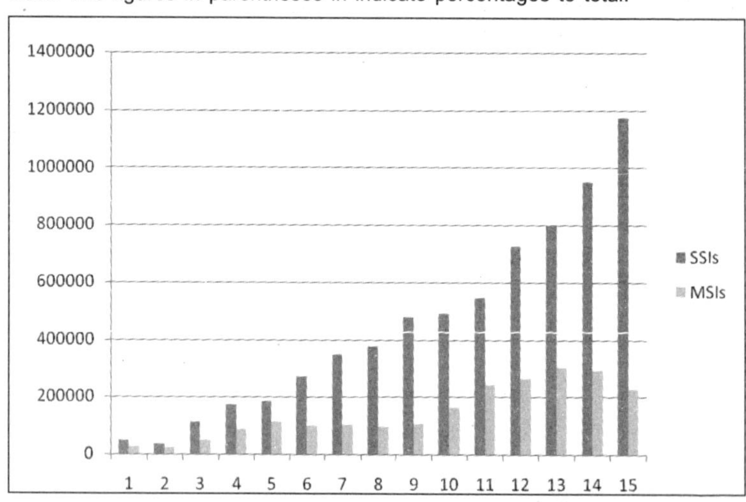

Diagram 4.1 : Disbursements of APSFC to SSIs and MSIs in Pre-Reform Period

The SSI sector, being identified as priority sector due to several advantages associated with it, The APSFC appears to have been giving a special trust to the financing of small scale industries, especially since 1976-77. This may be largely due to the policy reorientation of the Government for promotion of SSI sector to achieve the committed socio-economic objective.

It can be seen from Table 4.15 that SSI units obtained sanctions of Rs. 9,38,41 crores in 1976-77, while the amount sanctioned to these SSI units amounted to Rs. 1927,22,88 crores in 1990-91. On the other hand the MSI units received sanctions of Rs. 55,61 lakhs in 1976-77 and this stood at Rs. 53,84,56 crores in 1990-91. Thus, out of the total sanctions of 3199,01,95 crores for SSI units put together thus 87.17 per cent is claimed by SSI units while 12.83 per cent is claimed by MSI units during the pre-reform period.

In respect of disbursements out the total amount of Rs. 953,40,38 crores disbursed to both SSI units and MSI units put together, while the SSI units accounted 70.45 percent, the MSI units claimed just 29.55 of total disbursements.

Amounts Sanctions and Disbursements to SSI and MSI Units During Post-Reform Period

The data relating the amount sanctioned and disbursed to SSI units and MSI units during post-reform period are shown in table 4.16.

Table 4.16 : APSFC Assistance to SSIs & MSI Units During Post-Reform Period

(Amount in Rs. 000)

	SANCTIONS			DIBURSEMENTS		
Year	SSIs	MSI	Total	SSIs	MSI	Total
1	2	3	4	5	6	7
1991-92	1601189	454816	2056005	1698603	271080	1969683
	(77.88)	(22.12)	(100.00)	(86.24)	(13.76)	(100.00)
1992-93	1547521	342446	1889967	899873	361936	1261809
	(81.88)	(18.12)	(100.00)	(71.32)	(28.68)	(100.00)

1	2	3	4	5	6	7
1993-94	786966	153753	940719	662686	136777	799463
	(83.66)	(16.34)	(100.00)	(82.89)	(17.11)	(100.00)
1994-95	1107040	290051	1397091	607688	256380	864068
	(79.24)	(20.76)	(100.00)	(70.33)	(29.67)	(100.00)
1995-96	1439742	360373	1800115	837648	323186	1160834
	(79.98)	(20.02)	(100.00)	(72.16)	(27.84)	(100.00)
1996-97	1212661	309410	1522071	852569	268911	1121480
	(79.67)	(20.33)	(100.00)	(76.02)	(23.98)	(100.00)
1997-98	1531221	493503	2024724	996300	315004	1311304
	(75.63)	(24.37)	(100.00)	(75.98)	(24.02)	(100.00)
1998-99	2024679	660042	2684721	2024679	398516	2423195
	(75.41)	(24.59)	(100.00)	(83.55)	(16.45)	(100.00)
1999-00	2799792	552106	3351898	2097521	544541	2642062
	(83.529)	(16.471)	(100.00)	(79.39)	(20.61)	(100.00)
2000-01	2376026	1543078	3919104	2091858	736104	2827962
	(60.63)	(39.37)	(100.00)	(73.97)	(26.03)	(100.00)
2001-02	2330969	1569603	3900572	1816542	1268400	3084942
	(59.76)	(40.24)	(100.00)	(58.88)	(41.12)	(100.00)
2002-03	2322363	1526429	3848792	1819189	1190987	3010176
	(60.34)	(39.66)	(100.00)	(60.43)	(39.57)	(100.00)
2003-04	2293826	1400866	3694692	1701837	1129711	2831548
	(62.08)	(37.92)	(100.00)	(60.10)	(39.90)	(100.00)
2004-05	2312556	1820847	4133403	2023602	1461359	3484961
	(55.95)	(44.05)	(100.00)	(58.07)	(41.93)	(100.00)
2005-06	2507111	2473967	4981078	2098741	2117443	4216184
	(50.33)	(49.67)	(100.00)	(49.78)	(50.22)	(100.00)
Total	28193662	13951290	42144952	22229336	10780335	33009671
	(66.90)	(33.10)	(100.00)	(67.34)	(32.66)	(100.00)
Exponential	6.16*	16.90*		7.25*	16.47*	
Growth	t-(4.211)	t-(7.313)		t-(3.497)	t-(8.238)	

*Significant at 1 per cent level.

Source: Annual Reports of APSFC.

Note: The figures in parentheses in indicate percentages to total.

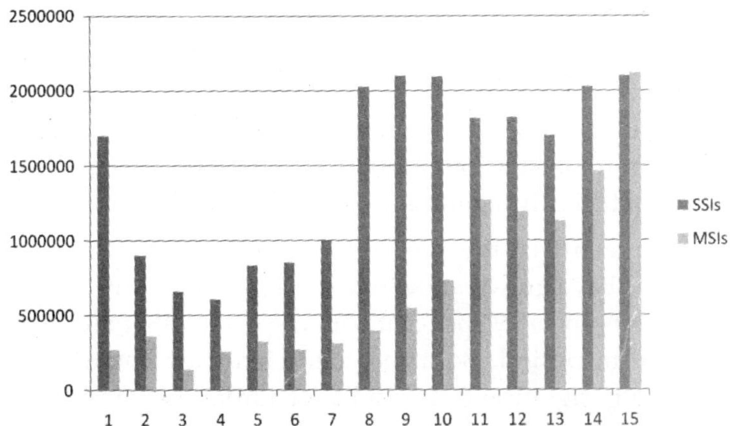

Diagram 4.2 : Disbursements of APSFC to SSIs and MSIs in Post-Reform Period

As can been from the table that, while the sanctions to SSI units amounted to Rs. 2819,36,62 crores these sanctions to MSI units stood at only Rs. 1395,12,90 crores during the post-reform period thus out of the total sanctioned amount of Rs. 4214,49,52 crores to both the SSI units and MSI units combined together, the SSI units claimed 66.90 percent while the MSI units obtained 33.10 percent in the total disbursed amount during the post reform period.

Coming to the total disbursements of Rs. 3300,96,71 crores the SSI units claimed 67.34 percent while the medium MSI claimed 32.66 percent of the total. From this it may be concluded that the policies and strategies of SSIs have been aiming at to sub serve the larger national objective of rapid industrial growth.

Growth of Sanctions to SSI and MSI Units

The growth of sanctions made by APSFC to SSI and MSI units have been examine for pre reform period and post reform period. The growth has been examined by estimating exponential growth rates. The result of the estimation of the exponential growth rate equation for sanctions is given in Table 4.7. As can be seen form the table in the pre-reform period the growth rate of sanctions is 22.37 per cent and is statistically significant with respect to SSI units. Similarly the growth rate of sanctions is worked out to be 12.14 per cent and is statistically significant with respect to MSI units.

The result of the post-reform period indicates that sanctions have grown at the rate of 6.16 per cent with respect to SSI units and 16.90 per cent with respect to MSI units in the pre reform period. Both the coefficients are found to be statistically significant. As can be seen from these results the sanctions have shown a higher growth rate in post reform period with respect to MSI units.

Growth of Disbursements to SSI units and MSI Units

The growth of disbursements effected by APSFC have been examined or pre-reform period and post reform period, by estimating the exponential growth rates. The results of the estimation of the exponential growth rate equation are given in Table 4.8. It is clear from the table the growth rate of disbursements is 22.21 per cent in re reform period, it is found to be 7.25 per cent in post reform period with respect to SSI units on the other hand the MSI units have registered a growth rate of 17.17 per cent in the pre reform period and 16.47 per cent in the post-reform indicating a marginal decline.

Thus the analysis of growth rates of sanctions and disbursements made by APSFC reveal that the MSI units have been shown higher growth rate with respect to sanctions and almost consistent growth rate with respect to disbursements when compared to MSI units. From this, it may be inferred that the sanctions and disbursements though are substantial with respect to SSIs, the percentage of sanctions has declined. On the other hand, in the case of MSIs the percentage share of sanctions and disbursements are gaining momentum.

Purpose-wise Assistance by APSFC

In order to meet the growing demand of industrial finances the corporation has started to engage itself in the promotion of entrepreneurship. It sponsored the entrepreneurial development programme jointly with APITCO, NISIET, etc. It has started organizing the EDPs on its own from 1989-90. Accordingly, it selects the potential entrepreneurs on specific procedure and trains them in all capacities of the enterprise establishment and management. The corporation embarked upon the task of building up a travel entrepreneurial base. It extends financial support to the emerging entrepreneurs also. The corporation extends purpose-wise assistance. The categories of purpose-wise assistance is mention below are:

(I) New Projects,

(II) Expansion and diversification,

(III) Modernization and replacement,

(IV) Rehabilitation,

(V) Supplementation, and VI).power generation.

The purpose wise assistance extended by the corporation to MSIs is provided in Table 4.17. The table shows the most favoured disposition of the corporation is towards the new projects in terms of both the number of units assisted and also the amount of assistance extended. The new projects accounted for 63.66 in total amount sanctioned to MSI industries. The expansion and diversification projects claimed the next largest share both in terms of number and the amount of sanctions consists of 34.75 per cent. This followed by supplementation assistance of 0.65 per cent. The power generation, rehabilitation, modernization and replacement claimed very little assistance both in terms of number and the amount during the period under study.

The corporation has started giving the purpose-wise assistance to small scale industries from the year 1989-90 only. Table 4.18 shows purpose-wise analysis of assistance sanctioned to the SSI sector. In the case of SSI sector the new projects claimed a large amount of assistance sanctioned by the corporation both in terms of number and amounts.

Table 4.17 : Purpose-wise Assitance Made by APSFC to MSIs

(Amount in Rs.000)

Year	New Project		Expansion & Diversification		Modernization/ Replace		Rehabilitation		Supplemental Assistant		Power generation		Total	
	No.	Amount	No.	Amount	No.	Amount	No.	Amount	No.	Amount	No.	Amount	No.	Amount
1989-90	95	263742	62	89303	10	10363	5	36554	2	4559	0	0	174	404521
1990-91	124	404430	50	105511	3	10928	4	4638	5	11077	0	0	186	536584
1991-92	166	325043	40	679661	4	11120	3	4694	13	27581	4	2185	230	1050284
1992-93	170	242922	25	32756	2	5048	2	1457	42	58396	2	2865	243	343444
1993-94	84	105048	19	33186	1	167	0	.0	4	4884	1	983	109	144268
1994-95	84	175500	40	104383	1	506	0	0	1	2740	3	1498	129	284627
1995-96	81	232663	37	13863	1	1161	1	5840	0	0	20	7260	140	260787
1996-97	87	242311	39	73957	1	1205	0	0	0	0	7	12184	134	329657
1997-98	135	360387	43	138826	1	230	0	0	0	0	3	1547	182	500990
1998-99	142	503432	40	179921	0	.0	0	0	0	0	1	8995	183	692348
1999-00	151	387993	55	239173	0	0	0	0	0	0	1	770	207	627936
2000-01	220	1152510	56	375362	0	0	0	0	0	0	3	998	279	1528870
2001-02	207	881673	132	740805	2	9795	0	0	0	0	0	0	341	1632273
2002-03	285	1077321	109	557870	0	.0	0	0	0	0	0	0	394	1635191
2003-04	282	1197691	109	506039	0	0	0	0	0	0	0	0	391	1703730
2004-05	238	1202831	111	856583	2	13900	0	0	0	0	0	0	351	2073314
2005-06	305	1909497	136	10936.91	0	0	0	0	0	0	0	0	441	3003188
Totals	**2856**	**10664994 (63.66)**	**1103**	**5820890 (34.75)**	**28**	**64423 (0.38)**	**15**	**53183 (0.32)**	**67**	**109237 (0.65)**	**45**	**39285 (0.23)**	**4114**	**16752012 (100.00)**

Source: Annual Reports of APSFC

Note: The figures in parentheses indicate percentages to total.

Table 4.18 : Purpose-wise Assitance Made by APSFC to SSIs

(Amount in Rs.000)

Year	New Project		Expansion & Diversification		Modernization/ Replace		Rehabilitation		Supplemental Assistant		Power generation		Total	
	No.	Amount	No.	Amount	No.	Amount	No.	Amount	No.	Amount	No.	Amount	No.	Amount
1989-90	4859	1257208	301	166652	27	5758	13	20085	0	0	44	6713	5244	1456416
1990-91	8422	1731219	201	105503	26	6832	440	53640	46	14996	88	20504	9223	1932694
1991-92	4250	1437247	142	134662	23	9818	2	2245	34	22995	49	13559	4500	1620526
1992-93	2696	1217897	155	117743	6	7271	10	14386	164	191853	29	8954	3060	1558104
1993-94	1035	628724	63	76120	11	7202	8	10850	61	24685	9	6856	1187	754437
1994-95	952	842362	107	229750	2	1820	4	7814	5	991	44	8245	1114	1090982
1995-96	985	1152581	132	260744	2	15451	3	7861	8	1554	88	38348	1218	1476539
1996-97	959	1128129	123	173054	0	0	0	0	6	3307	35	10641	1123	1315131
1997-98	1030	135725	140	262752	1	238	0	0	0	.0	27	11858	1198	410573
1998-99	1004	1803963	125	313836	2	3990	0	0	0	0	14	3660	1145	2125449
1999-00	1526	2786526	151	379087	0	0	0	0	1	038	7	1983	1685	3167634
2000-01	1351	1976718	172	458153	0	0	0	0	1	870	5	1879	1529	2437620
2001-02	609	1446148	469	1022099	1	4676	0	0	1	1900	3	636	1083	2475459
2002-03	742	1651344	211	905870	0	0	0	0	0	0	0	.0	953	2557214
2003-04	597	1770108	245	831008	0	0	0	0	0	0	0	0	842	2601116
2004-05	576	1782004	221	777421	2	7591	0	0	0	0	0	0	799	2567016
2005-06	448	1840199	260	1014806	0	0	0	0	0	0	0	0	708	2855005
Total	**32041**	**24588102 (78.88)**	**3218**	**7229260 (22.31)**	**103**	**70647 (0.22)**	**480**	**116881 (0.36)**	**327**	**263189 (0.81)**	**442**	**133836 (0.41)**	**36611**	**32401915 (100.00)**

Source: Annual Reports of APSFC

Note: The figures in parentheses indicate percentages to total.

The new projects claimed 75.88 per cent of the total sanctions out of the 32,041 total units. The expansion and diversification projects claimed 22.31 consisting of 3218. Supplemental assistance received significant amount of share 0.81 consisting of 327. It is interesting to note that the power generation got more assistance in terms of number of units compared to the supplemental assistance units. It is disheartening to note that rehabilitation and modernization/ replacements are getting lesser amounts of sanctions.

It is clear from Tables 4.17 and 4.18 which are representing MSIs and SSIs purpose-wise analysis assistance from APSFC. In the purpose wise analysis new projects, expansions and diversification, supplemental assistance receiving more amount of sanctions from the corporation. However, rehabilitation and power generation claimed fewer amount of sanctions to MSI. In the case of SSIs modernization/replace, and rehabilitation received less amount of sanctions.

The industrial finance made by corporation is remarkable contribution, in the prevailing environment of industrial development in the State. The Industry-wise assistance reveals that a substantial amount of sanctions and disbursements are effected to both traditional and modern industries. The assistance has been given to SSI units and to MSI units are quite impressive. The purpose-wise amount given by the corporation indicates that it is promoting the expanding of different types of services. Thus the scenario of flow of funds from the corporation indicates that the corporation is shouldering a lions share in extending financial assistance to industries in the state of Andhra Pradesh. In order to sustain the same trend of assistance to the industries the corporation has to maintain its performance in terms of sanctions, disbursements and recoveries. In this context an attempt has been made in the following chapter to evaluate APSFC performance during pre and reform periods.

Performance of APSFC

Introduction

APSFC has been a part and parcel of industrial development of Andhra Pradesh for six decades, catering its services particularly to small and medium scale sector in the state. Though most of the SFCs in the country, found it difficult to continue with the reforms, APSFC withstood the transition process with confidence and with a re-oriented corporate culture, work ethics and value system. APSFC has played the role of a facilitator and catalyst in encouraging entrepreneurship development. The Corporation attained itself to the 2k mode and made the corporation 'de novo' with a series of well coordinated steps with sharp focus, team work relationship.

The APSFC is an entrepreneur friendly organization with strong bonds and providing all financial facilities under one roof. The APSFC is making MOUs with Commercial Banks for arranging working capital loans. The APSFC has a strong asset base, and has been in the leading position, among SFCs in the country in sanctions, and disbursements. The Corporation is also able to earn the profits. The record net profit of Rs. 13.15 crores in 2004-05, is a fitting prelude to the

Golden Jubilee Celebrations of November 2005. The net profit after tax reckoned an increase of 30 per cent by 2006.

The APSFC has achieved a major breakthrough particularly in the year 2004-2005 on the cost front. The pre-payment of refinance installment to SIDBI helped the Corporation to achieve average borrowing cost which declined from 10.47 per cent to 10.14 per cent at the end of the fiscal year. The achievement in the key result areas of Sanctions and Disbursements are also all time high.

Another significant achievement of APSFC is in respect of Non-Performing Assets (NPAs). The recoveries attempted through planned and coordinated efforts, constant monitoring of the assets, the 'One Time Settlement Scheme' and quick sale seized units helped the Corporation to minimize the NPAs. APSFC has also set itself to achieve the ambitious targets in the key operational areas and to keep in view the priorities laid down in the State Government's Industrial Investment 2010. APSFC, with its dedicated and motivated work force, is confident to march forward in the industrial development of Andhra Pradesh. APSFC which has been keeping its lead position in succession among all the Sate Financial Corporations for the fifth year. The Corporation has received the FAPCCI Award, and "Best All Round Perfect Ramamurthy Silver Rolling Trophy- instituted by M/s.VBC Industries limited in 2005.

In this chapter an attempt is made to analyse the performance of APSFC in resource mobilization, sanctions and disbursements with a focus on recoveries and profits earned.

Resources Mobilisation of APSFC

The resources of the APSFC's share capital during the pre-reform period and post-reform periods are discussed below under three points of time 1976-77, 1990-91 and 2005-06.

Share Capital

The share capital of APSFC for the year 1976-77 is shown in table 5.1.

Table 5.1 : Share Capital of APSFC in 1976-77

(Rs. in lakhs)

Sl No.	Name of the Party	Number of Shares held Rs. 100/- each	Total paid-up capital (Rs.)	%
1.	Government of Andhra Pradesh	1,20,000	1,20,00,000	48.00
2.	IDBI	70,000	70,00,000	28.00
3.	Scheduled and Commercial Banks	23,925	23,92,500	9.57
4.	Insurance Companies, Instrument Trust and other financial institutions	22,415	22,41,500	8.98
5.	Co-operative Banks	5,580	5,58,000	2.23
6.	Individual share holders	8,080	8,08,000	3.23
	Total	**2,50,000**	**2,50,00,000**	**100.00**

Source: APSFC Annual Report 1976-77.

As can be seen from the table, the paid-up share capital of the Corporation at the end of 31st March, 1977 was Rs. 250 lakhs. To further augment the resources of the Corporation, it was decided to issue additional shares for Rs. 128 lakhs to be subscribed by the Government of Andhra Pradesh and IDBI in equal proportions. Although, the entire additional share capital of Rs. 128 lakhs has been received during the year under review, shares have been allotted to the Government of Andhra Pradesh and IDBI during the current year. The total paid-up share capital of the Corporation of Rs. 250 lakhs at the end of 31st March, 1977 is held by the Government of Andhra Pradesh, Industrial Development Bank of India, Insurance Companies, Banks etc. as detailed hereunder.

The resources of the APSFC during the year 1990-91 are presented below. The share capital of APSFC for the year 1990-91 is shown in Table 5.2. The Authorized Share Capital of the Corporation is Rs. 100 Crores, divided into shares of Rs 100 each. The Corporation raises two classes of Share Capital viz., Share Capital and Special Share Capital. The

Subscribed and Paid-up Share Capital of the Corporation excluding Special Share Capital as on 31st March 1991 stood at Rs. 3181.25 1akhs.

Table 5.2 : Share Capital of APSFC in 1990-91

(Rs. in lakhs)

Sl No.	Name of the Party	Number of Shares held Rs. 100/- each	Total paid-up capital (Rs.)	%
1.	Government of Andhra Pradesh	15,60,625	1560.625	49.06
2.	IDBI of India	15,60,625	1560.625	49.06
3.	Scheduled Banks	24.295	24.295	0.76
4.	Insurance Companies, PF Trusts & Other Institutions	25,835	25,835	0.81
5.	Co-operative Banks	5,580	5,580	0.18
6.	Industrial Shareholders	4,290	4,290	0.13
	Total	**31,81,250**	**31,81,250**	**31,81,250**

Source: APSFC Annual Report 1990-91

Details of the pattern of shareholdings held by Government of Andhra Pradesh, Industrial Development Bank of India (IDBI), Scheduled Banks, Insurance Companies, Co-operative Banks and individuals are given below. In the financial year 1990-91, an amount of Rs. 2310 lakhs has been allocated between State Government and IDBI in equal proportions towards Share Capital from out of the Share Capital Pending Allocation Account.

During this year, a sum of Rs. 495 lakhs was received from the State Government towards Loan in lieu of Share Capital as against Rs. 495 lakhs received in 1989-90 towards Share Capital. An amount of Rs. 491 lakhs was received during this year from the Industrial Development Bank of India as Additional Refinance in lieu of Share Capital (previous year Rs. 495 lakhs). This is the matching contri-bution in order to help the Corporation to service the enlarged capital more effectively.

The resources of the APSFC during the year 2005-06 are presented below. The share capital of APSFC for the year 2005-06 is shown in Table 5.3.

Table 5.3 : Share Capital of APSFC in 2005-06

(Rs. In lakhs)

Sl.No.	Shares held by	Equity share Capital	Special Capital	Total	% of holding
1.	State Govt.	5,751.087	556.375	6,307.462	68.40
2.	IDBI	2,330.987	556.375	2,887.362	31.31
3.	LIC of India	21.655	-	21.655	0.23
4.	Individuals, Co-op. banks PF trust etc.	5.511	-	5.511	0.06
	Total	**8,109.240**	**1,112.750**	**9,221.990**	**100.00**

Source: APSFC Annual Report 2005-06.

As can be seen from the table, the per centage share holding of the State Government is 68.4 per cent while that of IDBI is 31.31 per cent. The per centage of share holding of LIC of India is 0.23 per cent, while that of individuals, Co-operative Banks PF trust etc is 0.06 per cent.

Strategic Tie UP with other Institutions

The Corporation has entered in to a tie-up with commercial banks viz., Andhra Bank, State Bank of Hyderabad and Bank of India for co-financing and joint financing of Small and Medium Entrepreneurs (SMEs). These tie-ups are expected to help the entrepreneurs for securing the working capital facilities much faster and also to secure higher volume of term loans in large projects. The Corporation has also entered into MOU with Life Insurance Corporation. The APSFC has also signed a tie-up with IFCO Tokyo General Insurance (ITGI).

In order to ensure integrated and speedy flow of credit to SMEs, the APSFC has entered into an alliance with Bank of India on 27th January, 2006. The alliance is meant to provide easy facility of working capital for all the assisted units. Since APSFC is a term loan lending institution, entrepreneurs are required to approach commercial banks for their working capital requirements. The SME units previously used to face difficulty in securing timely and adequate working capital funds from commercial banks. The alliance of the Corporation with commercial banks would ensure an integrated package of financial requirement of industrial concerns. While APSFC can sanction term loans of up to Rs. 5 crores, the alliances with banks enables it to participate in larger loan sanctions in projects which require more than Rs. 5 crores of term loan.

Life Insurance Corporation of India and the Andhra Pradesh State Financial Corporation have come together for a tie up for distribution of life insurance products. The APSFC is a leading state level financial institution and an autonomous corporation while LIC of India is a dominant player in the insurance market. The LIC so far has tied up with 655 corporate agents through corporate agencies for life insurance products. This strategic tie in the financial service sector of the State and branches of APSFC facilitates to cover the wealth management needs of the customers.

From the foregoing analysis, it may be inferred that the Corporation has been relatively reducing its borrowing from other sources and raising its own funds through shares and debentures, besides the assistance from the State Government of Andhra Pradesh. In addition the SIDBI also has been assisting considerably to raise the funds of APSFC in view of increasing demands of entrepreneurs in the era of rapid industrialization scenario.

Applications Received by the Corporation

In any financial institution the demand for the assistance is indicated by the number of applications received. In the performance of the Corporation, the applications considered for assistance and amount sanctioned play an important role. It is in this context, an analysis has been made regarding loan applications received by the Corporation. The data relating to the total number of applications dealt with, applications rejected, applications considered for assistance and pending applications during the pre-reform period are shown in Table 5.4.

Table 5.4 : APSFC: Loans Applications Anlysis During 1976-1991

(Rs. In lakhs)

Year	Applications consider Assistance	Applications Rejected	Pending Applications	Applications Dealt	Amount sanctioned
1976-77	1023	200	252	1475	149502
1977-78	1396	186	200	1782	201890
1978-79	1479	183	143	1805	294114
1979-80	2117	180	363	2660	373865
1980-81	97	207	339	643	427567
1981-82	1523	240	365	2128	543478
1982-83	2488	237	424	3149	497879
1983-84	1877	163	664	2704	730872
1984-85	1837	557	196	2590	893580
1985-86	2200	164	196	2560	1063887
1986-87	2597	315	266	3178	1325151
1987-88	3657	324	580	4561	1318441
1988-89	3658	465	363	4486	1775680
1989-90	6703	308	701	7712	2614128
1990-91	10264	433	617	11314	3575578
Total	**42916 (81.36)**	**4162 (7.89)**	**5669 (10.75)**	**52747 (100.00)**	**15785612**

Source: APSFC Annual Reports

It is evident from the table that the number of applications dealt with in the year 1976-77 was 1475, while the number of applications dealt with in the year 1990-91 was 11,314 indicating an impressive increase. Out of the 52,747 total number of applications dealt with during the pre-reform period 81.36 per cent applications were considered for assistance, while 7.89 per cent applications were rejected by the APSFC. The pending applications accounted for 10.75 per cent.

The correlation coefficient between applications dealt with and applications considered for assistance is also calculated. There is positive correlation between the two variables. The correlation co-efficient is 0.99 and found to be statistically significant.

The data relating to the number of applications dealt with, applications received, applications considered and pending applications during the post-reform period are shown in Table 5.5.

Table 5.5 : APSFC: Loans Applications Anlysis During 1991-2006

(Rs. In lakhs)

Year	Applications consider Assistance	Applications Rejected	Pending Applications	Applications Dealt	Amount sanctioned
1991-92	6717	732	1003	8452	3127150
1992-93	3936	777	303	5016	2433143
1993-94	1511	422	316	2249	1079011
1994-95	1419	133	127	1679	1783601
1995-96	1561	171	122	1854	2464937
1996-97	1440	179	170	1789	2109725
1997-98	1505	168	155	1828	2542343
1998-99	1485	129	98	1712	3503947
1999-00	1968	181	148	2297	4322394
2001-01	1371	67	36	1474	4784728
2001-02	1353	79	NA	1432	3900572
2002-03	1262	59	21	1342	5087203
2003-04	1202	67	28	1297	5388582
2004-05	1170	56	46	1242	6538206
2005-06	1500	325	NA	1825	3223831
Total	**29400 (82.77)**	**3545 (9.98)**	**2573 (7.24)**	**35518 (100)**	**52289373**

Source: APSFC Annual Reports

As can be seen from the table, the number of applications dealt with in the year 1991-92 was 8452, while the number of applications dealt with in the year 2005-06 was 1825. Out of 35,518 applications dealt with, 82.78 per cent applications were considered for assistance, while 9.98 per cent applications were rejected by the corporation during this period. The pending applications accounted for 7.24 per cent. The correlations co-efficient between applications dealt with and applications considered for assistance is calculated. There is a positive correlation between the two variables. The correlation co-efficient is 0.99 per cent and found to be statistically significant.

The above analysis leads to a conclusion that the Corporation has received more number of applications during the pre-reform period than in the post-reform period. It is also observed that there is significant and positive correlation between the applications dealt and the applications considered for assistance during both the pre-reform period and the post-reform period.

Size-wise Analysis of Loans Sanctioned During Pre-Reform Period

The Corporation sets the maximum limits of assistance from time to time that can be sanctioned to various kinds of industries with varying amounts of capital requirements. The over all loan limits of general loans given to corporate bodies has been progressively increasing keeping pace with the development process.

The size of the loan varies due to size of the unit, nature of the industry and type of organisation. The Corporation has been expanding its range of sanctions to different units. The data pertaining to size-wise classification of loans during the pre-reform period are presented in Table 5.6. To get clearer insights into the advances made by the Corporation, the loan ranges have been categorized into 11 sizes for analytical convenience, as below:

(1) up to Rs. 10,000
(2) Rs. 10,001 to Rs. 25,000
(3) Rs. 25,001 to Rs. 50,000
(4) Rs. 50,001 to Rs. 100,000
(5) Rs. 100,001 to Rs. 2,00,000
(6) Rs. 2,00,001 to Rs. 5,00,000
(7) Rs. 5,00,001 to Rs. 10,00,000
(8) Rs. 10,000,001 to Rs. 20,00,000
(9) Rs. 20,00,001 to Rs. 30,00,000
(10) Rs. 30,00,001 to Rs. 45,00,000
(11) Rs. 45,00,000 & above.

Table 5.6 : APSFC size-wise Classification of Number of Loans Sanctioned During 1976-77 to 1990-1991

Year	Up to 10000	10001 to 25000	25001 to 50000	50001 to 100000	100000 to 200000	200001 500000	500001 to 1000000	100001 to 2000000	2000001 to 3000000	3000001 to 4500000	4500000& above
1976-77	358	131	105	182	110	67	45	13	12	0	0
1977-78	290	329	192	187	251	56	51	21	19	0	0
1978-79	73	231	149	197	618	106	53	29	24	0	0
1979-80	63	602	299	275	571	167	72	48	20	0	0
1980-81	723	257	196	283	444	320	94	60	40	0	0
1981-82	29	95	199	198	563	535	159	27	63	0	0
1982-83	983	195	185	223	877	401	121	69	77	0	0
1983-84	2	132	121	150	796	376	116	108	76	0	0
1984-85	1	109	134	156	545	520	138	114	120	0	0
1985-86	7	277	198	170	508	678	103	114	89	21	35
1986-87	148	313	397	180	324	800	126	126	121	32	83
1987-88	50	244	1019	305	438	1097	275	105	37	28	59
1988-89	14	254	964	208	322	1228	266	50	149	86	117
1989-90	46	694	1943	269	417	1377	426	136	110	57	48
1990-91	108	1793	2632	1102	934	1711	786	164	87	39	58
Total	**2895**	**5656**	**8733**	**4085**	**7718**	**9439**	**2831**	**1184**	**1044**	**263**	**400**

Source : APSFC Annual Reports.

During the pre-reform period, particularly the range of Rs. 25,001 to Rs. 50,000, Rs. 1 lakhs to 2 lakhs have recorded more number of sanctions than the other categories. During the period between 1980-81 and 1990-91, the range of Rs. 2 lakhs to Rs. 5 lakhs particularly accounted for more number of sanctions than other size groups. The category of Rs. 25,001 to Rs. 50,000 and Rs. 1 lakhs to 2 lakhs also recorded considerable number of sanctions. However, the range of Rs. 30 lakhs to Rs. 45 lakhs accounted for less number of sanctions.

Size-wise Analysis Number of Loans Sanctioned During the Post-Reform Period

Table 5.7 presents the size-wise classification of number of loans sanctioned during the post-reform period. The category in the range of Rs. 5 lakhs to Rs. 10 lakhs, followed by Rs. 2 lakhs to Rs. 5 lakhs, Rs. 1 lakhs to 2 lakhs have accounted for 5746, 5657 and 4086 numbers respectively. The range of Rs. 45 lakhs and above recorded 2178 number of sanctions while the range of Rs. 25,001 to Rs. 50,000 has accounted for 2021 number of sanctions.

On the basis of Tables 5.6 and 5.7, it may be observed that the number of loans sanctioned in the range of less than Rs. 5 lakhs is more, when compared to number of loans sanctioned in the same range of less than Rs. 5 lakhs during the pre-reform period. On the other hand, the number of loans sanctioned in the range of more than Rs. 5 lakhs is more, when compared to the number of loans sanctioned in the same range of more than Rs. 5 lakhs during the post-reform period. From this, it may be inferred that there is an impressive growth in the number loan sanctioned in the range of above Rs 5 lakhs during post-reform period

APSFC Size-wise Classification of Loan Amounts During Pre-Reform and Post-Reform Period

The information relating to the size-wise classification of loan amounts sanctioned during pre-reform period i.e., 1976-77 to 1990-91 is presented in Table 5.8. As can be seen from the table, a grand total amount of Rs. 1371.54 crores has been sanctioned under various size categories by the APSFC. Out of this, as high as 21.31 per cent loans have been sanctioned

Table 5.7 : APSFC Size-wise Classification Number of Loans Sanctioned During 1991-92 to 2005-06.

Year	Up to 10000	10001 to 25000	25001 to 50000	50001 to 100000	100000 to 200000	200001 500000	500001 to 1000000	100001 to 2000000	2000001 to 3000000	3000001 to 4500000	4500000 & above	Year wise Total
1991-92	167	367	1305	405	421	1163	524	152	112	33	82	4731
1992-93	309	268	467	158	337	724	614	180	115	66	65	3303
1993-94	68	74	143	56	169	322	244	117	31	28	44	1296
1994-95	51	21	51	45	129	414	266	115	42	30	79	1243
1995-96	0	4	17	31	86	547	310	148	51	47	117	1358
1996-97	0	1	3	15	51	421	418	176	54	39	80	1258
1997-98	0	1	0	7	54	334	499	238	89	45	113	1380
1998-99	0	0	0	0	17	256	504	261	71	38	181	1328
1999-00	0	0	1	0	31	519	513	408	152	50	218	1892
2001-01	117	29	13	5	28	367	470	491	141	40	170	1871
2001-02	0	6	5	8	24	210	318	438	145	78	193	1425
2002-03	0	3	13	2	17	132	299	400	205	74	203	1348
2003-04	0	1	1	1	7	99	261	337	248	80	198	1233
2004-05	0	1	0	0	1	89	260	324	208	68	199	1150
2005-06	0	0	2	0	2	60	246	301	230	72	236	1149
Size-wise Totals	**712**	**776**	**2021**	**733**	**1374**	**5657**	**5746**	**4086**	**1894**	**788**	**2178**	**25965**

Source: Annual Reports of APSFC.

Table 5.8 : APSFC Size-wise Classification of Loans Amount Sanctioned During 1976-77 to 1990-1991

(Amount in Rs'000)

Year	Upto 10000	10001 to 25000	25001 to 50000	50001 to 100000	100000 to 200000	200001 500000	500001 to 1000000	100001 to 2000000	2000001 to 3000000	3000001 to 4500000	4500000& above	Year-wise Total
1976-77	2884	2403	3788	14553	17162	22839	31580	20882	33411	0	0	14902
1977-78	2423	4511	7277	14527	37452	19555	35591	29114	52897	0	0	203347
1978-79	644	3834	5546	14848	89223	34911	39349	38431	67328	0	0	294114
1979-80	506	11374	10009	23009	95833	56482	56493	64352	55807	0	0	373865
1980-81	507	5154	6964	20763	72630	101556	68122	83013	108055	0	0	466764
1981-82	250	1936	7263	15111	97051	159071	96795	90753	147717	0	0	615947
1982-83	2151	3823	6781	15903	151412	127929	83477	97482	207491	0	0	696449
1983-84	019	2558	4638	11196	131989	130221	84174	149129	216948	0	0	730872
1984-85	010	2385	5136	11870	90453	185085	101198	169605	327838	0	0	893580
1985-86	058	6143	7373	12080	86479	212097	75774	165306	240707	71422	186448	1063887
1986-87	1218	6234	15707	13123	59176	236880	94296	176229	146617	105874	46977	902331
1987-88	425	4534	39767	19240	68504	301676	177266	151742	93480	101147	315434	1273215
1988-89	123	5170	40184	15119	47345	348250	171411	44425	222039	218152	543308	1655526
1989-90	416	15259	79459	18852	61884	434350	289803	200205	276859	279408	279408	1935903
1990-91	879	35831	115898	76398	135419	551238	463090	221449	221449	140250	498266	2460167
Size-wise Totals	12513 (0.09)	111149 (0.81)	355790 (2.59)	296592 (2.16)	1242012 (9.06)	2922140 (21.31)	1868419 (13.62)	1702117 (12.41)	2418643 (17.63)	916252 (6.68)	1869841 (13.63)	13715469 (100.00)

Source: Annual Reports of APSFC.

in the size-wise classification of Rs. 2 lakhs to Rs 5 lakhs, followed by 17.63 per cent in the category of Rs. 20 lakhs to Rs. 30 lakhs. It is interesting to note from Table 5.8, that no loans have been sanctioned in the two size categories viz. Rs. 30 lakhs to 45 lakhs and above Rs. 45 lakhs up to 1984-85. The loans in these two categories gained momentum only since 1985-86. It is much more interesting to note that the loans sanctioned in the size categories of Rs. 45 lakhs and above, obtained as high as 13.63 per cent of the total sanctioned amount in spite of the late start.

The data relating to the size wise classification of loans sanctioned by APSFC during post-reform period i.e. 1991-92 to 2005-06 are shown in Table 5.9. As can be seen from Table 5.9, a total amount of Rs. 4549.69 crores has been sanctioned by APSFC during post-reform period. Out of this gross amount sanctioned, as high as 53.74 per cent went to the categories of Rs. 45 lakhs and above, followed by 14.09 per cent belonging to the category of Rs. 10 lakhs to Rs. 20 lakhs. The total loan sanctioned in the category of Rs. 20 lakhs to Rs. 30 lakhs occupied the third position.

A look at the size-wise classification of loans sanctioned during pre- and post-reform period revealed that more than half of the gross loans sanctioned by the APSFC went to the size wise classification of Rs. 45 lakhs and above category. From this, it may be inferred that of the total assistance sanctioned by APSFC, a major part is going to the highest category range that is Rs. 45 lakhs and above.

APSFC Sanctions and Disbursements During Pre-Reform Period

Table 5.10 shows the amounts of year-wise financial assistance in the form of sanctions and disbursements made by the APSFC to all sectors during the pre-reform period. As can be seen from Table 5.10, the sanctions have increased from Rs. 1290.90 lakhs in 1976-77 to Rs. 23010.44 lakhs in 1990-91. The sanctions have gone up continuously till 1990-91 except in the year 1982-83 and 1987-88 which registered a negative growth over previous year with -8.93, -0.39 respectively.

Table 5.9 : APSFC Size-wise Classification of Loans Amount Sanctioned Excluding Bridge & Special Loans During 1991-92 to 2005-06.

(Amount in Rs. '000)

Year	Up to 10000	10001 to 25000	25001 to 50000	50001 to 100000	100000 to 200000	200001 500000	500001 to 1000000	100001 to 2000000	2000001 to 3000000	3000001 to 4500000	4500000& above	Year-wise Total
1991-92	1315	8767	50958	28568	62106	381345	354503	223680	285765	123832	550981	2071820
1992-93	2114	5457	18570	12093	50863	235889	424539	260767	288136	233683	369437	1901548
1993-94	653	1441	5774	4099	26244	103238	161491	163076	80147	106128	246414	898705
1994-95	255	393	2141	3462	21079	151777	204584	183849	111621	113398	583050	1375609
1995-96	0	066	683	2435	14366	207324	244847	245613	129786	176200	840777	1862097
1996-97	0	118	148	1141	8037	169107	324969	297784	137838	141859	563887	1644888
1997-98	0	024	0	548	9551	121438	391272	392820	238190	171516	807731	2133090
1998-99	0	0	0	0	2598	97400	382285	426934	192286	146046	1551132	2798681
1999-00	0	0	038	0	4792	171149	317079	607833	405225	194807	2009242	3710165
2001-01	0	584	579	353	4351	126092	335646	739461	377250	152416	2242384	3979116
2001-02	0	130	171	621	3295	78846	255163	692348	378566	298773	2404634	4112547
2002-03	0	059	500	134	2350	55060	247057	636950	527953	286290	2445318	4201671
2003-04	0	024	045	100	1236	43543	256508	542535	646854	309017	2541664	4341526
2004-05	0	013	0	0	140	40703	198048	524974	537062	264253	3038457	4603650
2005-06	0	0	065	0	366	28267	229959	473571	598775	275784	4255011	5861798
Size-wise Total	**4337 (0.01)**	**17076 (0.04)**	**79672 (0.18)**	**53554 (0.12)**	**211374 (0.46)**	**2011178 (4.42)**	**4327950 (9.51)**	**6412195 (14.09)**	**4935454 (10.85)**	**2994002 (6.58)**	**24450119 (53.74)**	**45496911 (100.00)**

Source: Annual Reports of APSFC.

Table 5.10 : APSFC Effective Sanctions and Disbursements During 1976-77 to 1990-91

(Rs. in lakhs)

Year	Sanctions	Growth over Previous year	Disburse-ments	Growth over Previous year	GAP Between sanction disburse-ments
1976-77	1290.90		735.99		554.91
1977-78	1839.70	29.83	1090.15	32.49	749.55
1978-79	2714.57	32.23	166.78	-553.65	2547.79
1979-80	3532.32	23.15	2730.06	93.89	802.26
1980-81	4371.41	19.19	3089.13	11.62	1282.28
1981-82	5461.02	19.95	3741.06	17.43	1719.96
1982-83	5013.24	-8.93	4517.3	17.18	495.94
1983-84	6316.26	20.63	4785.33	5.60	1530.93
1984-85	6889.76	8.32	5937.2	19.40	952.56
1985-86	9355.23	26.35	7066.49	15.98	2288.74
1986-87	11706.22	20.08	7807.11	9.49	3899.11
1987-88	11660.76	-0.39	10248.93	23.83	1411.83
1988-89	15224.55	23.41	11323.56	9.49	3900.99
1989-90	16059.29	5.20	12784.15	11.43	3275.14
1990-91	23010.44	30.21	14473.91	11.67	8536.53
Total	**124445.67**		**90497.15**		**33948.52**

Source: Annual Reports of APSFC.

The total sanctions for this period account Rs. 124445.67 lakhs. On the other hand, the disbursements went up from Rs. 735.99 lakhs to Rs. 14473.91 lakhs in the pre reform period. Except in the year 1978-79, disbursements have registered positive growth rates in all the years of the pre reform period. From the above table it is also interesting to note that the gap between sanctions and disbursements have been more or less widening.

This hints at the need for identifying the specific reasons for this gap between sanctions and disbursements. The sanctions and disbursements during pre-reform period are shown in diagram 5.1.

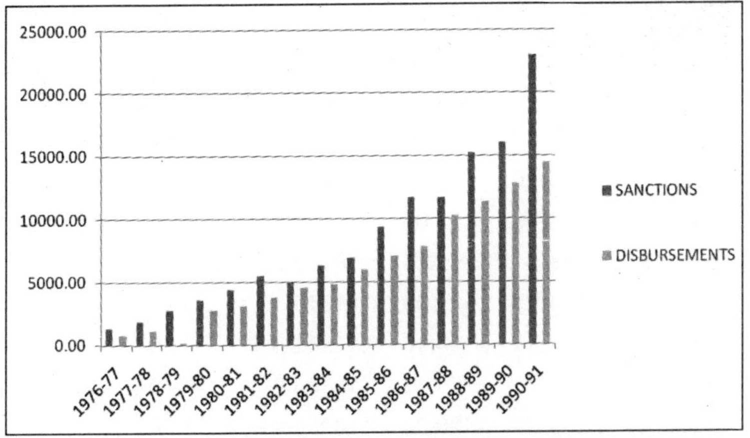

Diagram-5.1: Sanctions and Disbursements During Pre-Reform Period

APSFC Sanctions and Disbursements During Post-Reform Period

The data pertaining to sanctions and disbursements made by APSFC during the post-reform period is presented in Table 5.11. The sanctions have increased from Rs. 16,750.68 lakhs in 1992 to Rs. 44,851.48 lakhs by 2005-06 during the post-reform period. The Corporation has sanctioned significant amounts through out the period, except in the year 1998-99 (Rs. 2239.74 lakhs) which has shown a negative growth over the previous year. The total amount of sanctions during the period accounted for Rs. 30,5659.44 lakhs.

The table also shows the data pertaining to disbursements in the same period. The disbursements of the Corporation substantially increased from Rs. 1572.32 lakhs in 1991-92 to Rs 42172.45 lakhs by 2005-06. The total amount of disbursements worked out to be Rs. 30,5270.17 lakhs.

Table 5.11 : APSFC Effective Sanctions and Disbursements During 1991-92 to 2005-06

(Rs. in lakhs)

Year	Sanctions	Growth over Previous year	Disburse-ments	Growth over Previous year	GAP Between sanction disburse-ments
1991-92	16750.68	-37.37	1572.32	-820.54	15178.36
1992-93	9053.96	-85.01	13252.69	88.14	-
1993-94	9539.68	5.09	8206.7	-61.49	1332.98
1994-95	10163.01	6.13	8772.58	6.45	1390.43
1995-96	9994.26	-1.69	11680.76	24.90	-
1996-97	11676.1	14.40	11246.41	-3.86	429.69
1997-98	15595.95	25.13	13185.21	14.70	2410.74
1998-99	2239.74	-596.33	16250.41	18.86	-
1999-00	27674.89	91.91	26421.72	38.50	1253.17
2001-01	32238.3	14.16	28317.12	6.69	3921.18
2001-02	28170.15	-14.44	30849.42	8.21	-
2002-03	29970.72	6.01	30130.06	-2.39	-
2003-04	26728.35	-12.13	28324.87	-6.37	-
2004-05	31012.17	13.81	34887.45	18.81	-
2005-06	44851.48	30.86	42172.45	17.27	2679.03
Total	**305659.44**		**305270.17**		**28595.58**

Source: Annual Reports of APSFC.

The gap between sanctions and disbursements is not only declining but the disbursements exceeded the sanctions in some of the years. From this table it is observed that there are fluctuations in the growth rates of both sanctions and disbursements during the post reform period.

The foregone analysis gives a clear idea of sanctions and disbursements. The Corporation has been rising sanctions and disbursements quite impressively, and more particularly in the post-reform period. Sanctions and disbursements during post-reform period are shown in diagram 5.2.

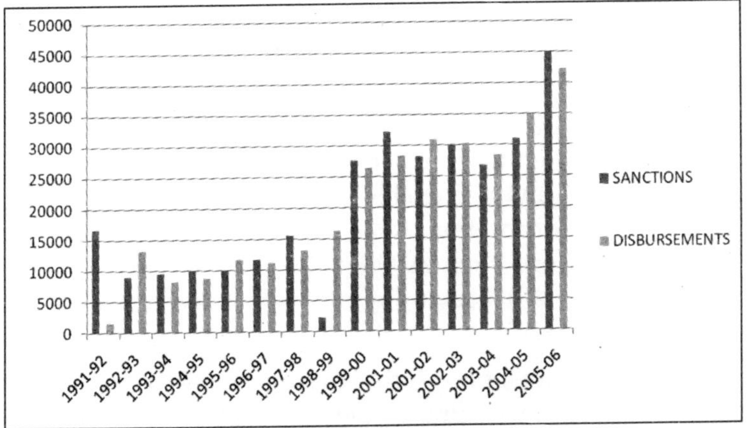

Diagram 5.2 : Sanctions and Disbursements During Post-Reform Period

Recoveries

The system of accounting was changed from the "mercantile system" to cash system for presenting the financial results with effect from 1st April, 1978 in the Corporation. The mercantile system of accounting which was followed by the Corporation right from its inception was replaced by a cash system of accounting' with a view to account for the income which was actually realized and expenditure which has actually been incurred to determine the financial results. It is viewed that the cash system of accounting would present the financial result of the Corporation in proper perspective as compared with the mercantile system of accounting. The Corporation has been initiating recovery action under the provisions of Andhra Pradesh Revenue Recovery Act (APRR Act) since 1984-85.

Recoveries of APSFC

Loan collection or loan repayments from the assisted units herein called recoveries indicate not only of the quality of lending operations of APSFC, but also in a way the performance of their assisted units. If the recoveries are encouraging, faster recycling of funds become possible which enable the Corporation to improve their disbursements. In fact, good collections from industrial debtors prepare the lenders psychologically to expand lending operations. Improvement in recoveries strengthens their owned funds, which in turn enhance their borrowing capacity. Timely recoveries of loans also enable the Corporation to repay the loans of the Corporation, which have been taken from the Apex Institutions such as the RBI, SEBI and IDBI. Thus, recoveries have a bearing almost in every phase of the working of APSFC.

As against this, poor recoveries of loans lead to adverse effects on the functioning of the Corporation. It results not only in the increased over dues from the assisted units, but also in shortage of funds for further lending and the consequent dependence on external agencies such as State Government, SIDBI and IDBI. It dims the Corporation prospects of raising funds from other sources and adversely affects their annual profits. Poor recoveries from some industrial debtors may sometimes have an impact on the morale of non-defaulters as well.

Recoveries from the assisted units constitute an important source of working funds of APSFC, and the availability of these funds facilitates disbursements. Further, recovery performance of APSFC is generally measured in terms of principal recoveries and interest amount collected in relation to loan outstanding. Hence, it is of interest to study the recovery performance of APSFC during the study period 1976-77 to 2005-06 covering the pre and post-reform periods. The data pertaining to recoveries for the pre-reform period are presented in Table 5.12. The recovery position of APSFC during pre-reform period is shown in diagram 5.3.

Recoveries and Share of Disbursements During Pre-Reform Period

Recoveries as per centage of disbursements indicate what part of the disbursements could be made out of loan collections. As can be seen from Table 5.12, the recoveries as per centage of disbursements are continuously increasing from year to year. Here, recoveries consist of recovery of principal and interest amount collected by the APSFC. It can be observed that there is a steady increase in recoveries as per centage of disbursements. It is interesting to note that recovery as per centage of disbursements is exceptionally high in the year 1978-79, and the recoveries amount is more than the disbursements.

Table 5.12 : Recovery Performance of APSFC's During Pre-Reform Period

(Rs. in lakhs)

Year	Disburse-ments	Recovery of Principal	% of Principal Recover In Dis-bursement	Interest Amount Collected	Total Recovery
1976-77	735.99	190.49	25.88	283.14	473.63
1977-78	1090.15	218.81	20.07	348.70	567.51
1978-79	166.78	602.71		209.28	811.99
1979-80	2730.06	587.64	21.52	481.74	1069.38
1980-81	3089.13	789.74	25.57	749.99	1539.73
1981-82	3741.06	1128.83	30.17	1004.47	2133.3
1982-83	4517.3	1564.28	34.63	1299.83	2864.11
1983-84	4785.33	2098.80	43.86	1594.93	3693.73
1984-85	5937.2	2279.77	38.40	2095.41	4375.18
1985-86	7066.49	2892.28	40.93	2455.39	5347.67
1986-87	7807.11	3296.55	42.22	2668.77	5965.32
1987-88	10248.93	3644.94	35.56	3239.02	6883.96
1988-89	11323.56	4659.61	41.15	3826.35	8485.96
1989-90	12784.15	5496.27	42.99	4871.96	10368.23
1990-91	14473.91	6346.57	43.85	5170.86	11517.43
Total	**90497.15**	**35797.29**		**30299.84**	**66097.13**

Source: Annual Reports of APSFC.

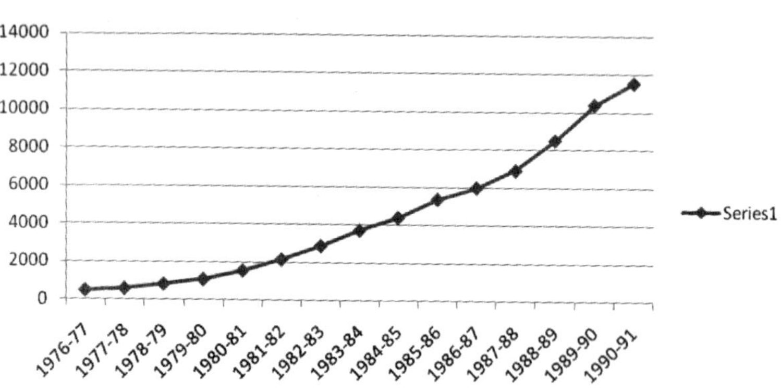

Diagram 5.3 : Recovery Position of APSFC in Pre-Reform Period

It can be seen from Table 5.12, that the recovery of principal amount has gone up from Rs. 190.49 lakhs to Rs. 6346 lakhs during the pre-reform period. The total amount of recovery of principal accounted for Rs. 35,797.29 lakhs. The rate of interest amount collected from the assisted units went up from Rs. 283.14 lakhs in 1976-77 to Rs. 5170.86 lakhs in 1990-91. The total amount of recoveries accounted for Rs. 66,271.46 lakhs during the pre-reform period. Here an attempt has been made to find the correlation between disbursements and recoveries in this period. The results indicated that the correlation co-efficient is 0.98 and this is found to be statistically significant and positively correlated.

Recoveries and Share of Disbursements During Post-Reform Period

During the post-reform period the total recovery amounts collected by the Corporation in the form of (i) Recoveries of principal and (ii) interest amount collected along with disbursements is shown in Table 5.13.

Table 5.13 : Recovery Performance of APSFC's During Post-Reform Period

(Rs. in lakhs)

Year	Disburse-ments	Recovery of Principal	% of Principal Recover In Dis-bursement	Interest Amount Collected	Total Recovery
1991-92	1572.32	7037.76	-	6376.75	13414.51
1992-93	13252.69	7859.47	59.30	8080.21	15939.68
1993-94	8206.7	10242.17	-	10265.19	20507.36
1994-95	8772.58	12130.59	-	1087.99	13218.58
1995-96	11680.76	10967.30	93.89	9162.51	20129.81
1996-97	11246.41	10403.48	92.50	9157.47	19560.95
1997-98	13185.21	11531.44	87.46	8661.95	20193.39
1998-99	16250.41	12873.93	79.22	9261.17	22135.1
1999-00	26421.72	13769.77	52.12	10048.32	23818.09
2001-01	28317.12	17597.78	62.15	11873.13	29470.91
2001-02	30849.42	20000.44	64.83	13825.46	33825.9
2002-03	30130.06	26362.97	87.50	14486.35	40849.32
2003-04	28324.87	31960.03	-	13061.71	45021.74
2004-05	34887.45	33110.55	94.91	12028.85	45139.4
2005-06	42172.45	35218.91	83.51	12995.13	48214.04
Total	**305270.2**	**261066.6**		**150372.2**	**411438.8**

Source: Annual Reports of APSFC.

The principal recoveries went up from Rs. 7037.76 lakhs in 1991-92 to Rs. 35,218.91 lakhs by 2005-06. The total amount of recovery of principal, accounted for Rs. 261,066.59 lakhs during this period. In the case of interest amount collected, the amount has gone up from Rs. 6,376.75 lakhs in 1991-92 to Rs. 12,995.13 lakhs during the post-reform period. Further, the total amount of recoveries stood at Rs. 13,413.75 lakhs in 1991-92, while the total amount of recoveries registered at Rs. 47,214.04 lakhs by 2005-06. The total recovery of (i) Principal amount and (ii) interest amount collected during the post-reform period amounted to Rs. 41,1455.62 lakhs. The recovery position of APSFC during the post-reform period is shown in diagram 5.4.

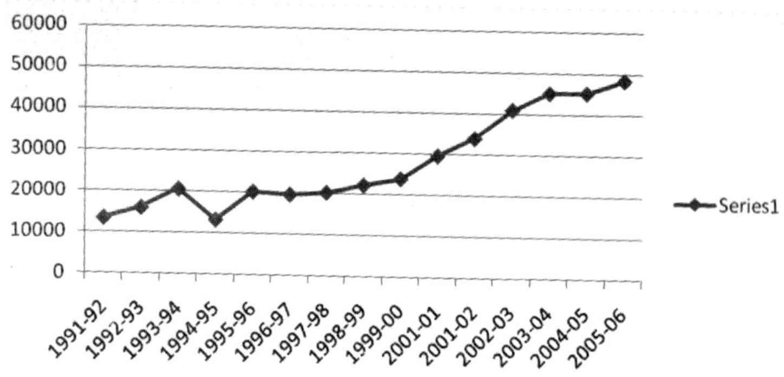

Diagram 5.4 : Recovery Position of APSFC in Post-Reform Period

An attempt is made to find out the association between disbursements and total recoveries. As such, the co-efficient of correlation is calculated between these two variables. The co-efficient of correlation is 0.91 and it is found to be positively correlated and statistically significant. The comparison of recoveries between pre-reform period and post-reform period reveals that the performance is quite impressive during the post-reform period.

Regression Analysis

The major objective of the analysis is to identify the recovery factors affecting the Disbursements (DISB) made by the APSFC. In this connection, Principal Recovery (PRC) and Interest Amount Collected (INTC) by the APSFC are taken as independent variables and the Disbursements made is treated as dependent variable. Both linear and log linear (Cobb-Doglous) functional forms are used in the estimation.

The association between the Disbursement (DISB) and Principal Recovery (PRC) or Interest Amount Collected (INTC) is generally measured by either correlation analysis or regression analysis. The correlation coefficient, represented by "r", indicates the type of association according to its sign and describes whether there is high or low association between the two variables considered. On the other hand, in the regression analysis the sign of the regression coefficient (referred by 'b' in the present study) dictates the type of association between the two variables. Further, the value of regression coefficient 'b' in the linear form indicates the change in the dependent variable, Disbursements (DISB) for one unit change in independent variable (PRC or INTC). The regression coefficient, 'b' in the log-linear form explains the per centage change in dependent variable for every one per cent change in the independent variable. The square of the correlation coefficient (r^2) measures the goodness of fit of the estimated functional form. One can establish a relation between correlation coefficient and regression coefficient:

$$b_{yx} = r_{yx} (\sigma_y / \sigma_x)$$

where σ_y = standard deviation of Disbursement (y) and

σ_x = standard deviation of x (PRC or INTC)

In order to test whether the ordinary lest square estimate of 'b' is significant or not (Ho: $b = 0$ against H1: $b \neq 0$), the Student's t-test is generally used. The test is based on the value of t-ratio computed from the estimated functional form of the computed t-ratios. They are, generally, given in the parentheses under the estimated value of regression coefficient.

The t - ratio of the regression coefficient of b is computed from the formula:

t - ratio = (OLS estimate of b/standard error of OLS estimate of b)

The computed results in terms of the estimated linear regression equation, Goodness of fit (r^2) and the t-ratios are given under standard format in Table 5.14 for pre-reform period, post-reform period and for the combined period separately.

The upper part of the table, presents the OLS results of linear functional relationship between DISB and PRC while the lower part of the table provides the OLS results of linear functional relationship between DISB and INTC. As mentioned earlier, in the case of linear form of the functions, the elasticities are to be computed from the estimated value of the regression coefficient. The formula involves the dependent variable as well as the independent variable. It means elasticity changes according to the pair of the values on *X* and *Y*. Generally, the researchers compute elasticity at the mean values of *Y* and *X*, (*Y* bar and *X* bar). The values of elasticities computed at these averages are presented in the upper part of the Table 5.16.

In the present analysis the following two variable liner regressions is used

$$Y_t = a + b\,X_t + u_t$$

where Y_t = Disbursement units by APSFC during the period t

$b = dy_t/dx_t$

X_t = PRC = Principal Recovery (in lakhs) by APSFC (or)

INTC = Interest amount collected (in lakhs) by APSFC and

u_t = Stochastic disturbances term

Here a and b will give marginal value of DISB with respect to PRC (or INTC)

The parameters a and b are estimated by the "Ordinary Least Squares (OLS)" method and the results are discussed in this section.

Log-linear form

In this section the log-linear (Double-log or Cobb-Douglas or Constant elasticity) form is used to estimate the relation between Disbursement (DISB) and Principle recovery PRC), and Interest collected (INTC).

Table 5.14 : Results of Estimated Linear Regression Equations During Pre-Reform (1976-77 to 1991-91), Post-Reform Period (1991-92 to 2005-2006) and Combined Period (1976-77 to 2005-06)

Period	Equation	r^2	F-value
Pre-reform period:			
	(a) **DISB** = 651.298 + 2.255* PRC	0.973	467.93
	(21.632) (2.049)		
	(b) **DISB** = 590.574 + 2.694* INTC	0.983	735.58
Post-reform period:			
	(a) **DISB** = 1355.105 + 1.091* PRC	0.77	47.89
	(0.435) (6.92)		
	(b) **DISB** = –6316.04 + 2.66* INTC	0.578	17.81
	(–0.099) (4.221)		
Combined period:			
	(a) **DISB** = 2946.348 + 1.35* PRC	0.862	174.54
	(2.66) (13.21)		
	(b) **DISB** = 871.565 + 2.046* INTC	0.751	84.39
	(0.51) (9.186)		

Note: (1) Figures in parenthesis indicate Student's t values.

(2) *Indicates level of significance at 5 per cent

$$\text{Log } Y_t = a + b\,X_t + U_t$$

where Y_t = DISB = disbursement by APSFC in period t

X_t = PRC Principle Recovery by APSFC or

INTC = Interest Amount Collected by APSFC during period t

U_t = Stochastic discordance term

In the function, b indicate elasticity of Disbursement with respect to INTC or PRC.

$$\text{Regression Coefficient} = \beta = d\,\text{DISB}/d\text{PRC}\left(\frac{\text{PRC}}{\text{DISB}}\right)$$

= Elasticity of DISB with respect of PRC in the log-liner functional relation between DISB and INTC

Similarly when INTC is used as independent variable instead of PRC then Regression coefficient = $b = d\,\text{DISB}/d$

$$\text{INTC}\left(\frac{\text{INTC}}{\text{DISB}}\right) = \text{Elasticity of DISB with respect of INTC.}$$

Table 5.15 : Results of Estimated Linear Regression Equations During Pre-Reform (1976-77 to 1991-91), Post-Reform Period (1991-92 to 2005-2006) and Combined Period (1976-77 to 2005-06)

Period	Equation	r^2	F-value
Pre-reform period:			
	(a) log DISB = 1.516 + 0.92* log PRC (1.244) (5.597)	0.707	31.33
	(b) log DISB = 0.42 + 1.091* log INTC (0.551) (10.401)	0.893	108.19
Post- reform period:			
	(a) log DISB = -2.773 + 1.294* log PRC (1.126) (5.063)	0.664	25.63
	(b) log DISB = 3.725 + 0.655* log INTC (1.266) (2.03)	0.241	4.12
Combined period:			
	(a) log DISB = 2.629 + 0.748* log PRC (3.692) (9.031)	0.744	81.56
	(b) log DISB = 2.081 + 0.846* log INTC (2.798) (9.186)	0.759	87.96

Note : Figures in parenthesies indicate Student's *t* values.

* Indicates level of significance at 5 per cent

The first regression equation in Table 5.14 presents the estimated value of intercept, the regression coefficient, their t-ratios as well as the goodness of fit and its F-ratio in the case of linear relationship between DISB and PRC. The value of the regression coefficient 2.26 indicates that one unit increase (or decrease) in PRC results in 2.26 units increase (or decrease) in DISB during the pre-reform period (1976-77 to 1990-91). The value is statistically significant at one per cent level. Further the value of goodness of fit (given under column r^2) indicates that 97 per cent of variation in Disbursement during the pre-reform period is explained by the variation in PRC alone. This result is also statistically significant at one per cent level according to F-test performed on goodness of fit. On the other hand, during post-reform period, the estimated value of regression coefficient is observed to be 1.09, that is, only 1.09 units increase (or decrease) in DISB is depicted for every one unit increase (or decrease) in PRC amount. Thus, the value of the regression coefficient in post-reform period is considerably lower than its counter part in pre-reform period. However, there are three common features:

(1) the association between disbursement and PRC is positive (or direct) in both the periods.

(2) The estimated linear regression equations in both the periods are statistically significant in terms of goodness of fit and

(3) the impact of PRC on Disbursement is relatively declined during the two periods of the study.

In contrast to the results obtained from the functional relationship between Disbursement (DISB) and Interest Amount Collected (INTC) indicates that the value of the regression coefficient is around 2.7 during both the periods (pre-reform as well as post-reform). It indicates that for every one unit (measured in Rs. lakhs) increase (or decrease) in INTC caused 2.7 units (measured in Rs. lakhs) increased (or decreased) in disbursement during both the periods. The explanatory power of INTC is higher than that of PRC during pre-reform period. About 98 per cent of variation is explained by INTC alone during this period.

During the combined period, (1976-77 to 2005-06) the regression coefficients are 1.35 (when DISB is regressed on PRC) and 2.05 (when DISB is regressed on INTC).

Thus the estimated values of the regression coefficients are considerably higher when DISB is regressed on INTC than its counter part, regression coefficient when DISB is regressed on PRC during the two sub-periods as well as the combined period. From the linear empirical analysis, one can conclude that the impact of INTC is considerably higher than PRC on DISB during all the periods.

The results of log-linear form are presented in Table 5.15. The results can be compiled as in the lines of linear form with the exception of interpretation of regression coefficient. The coefficient of the variable measures elasticity in the log-linear form and the marginal values in the case of linear form. If one considers the *t*-ratios, goodness of fit and the F-ratios, the linear form performed very well than log-linear form in almost all the regression equations.

Strictly speaking, one can not compare the estimated values of regression coefficient of linear and log-linear forms as their properties are different. The linear form is variable elasticity form while log-linear form is constant elasticity form.

An attempt is also made to compute elasticities at mean values of the variables used in the analysis of linear functional form and these elasticities are given in the upper part of the Table 5.16. The lower part of the table contains elasticities directly derived from the log-linear form for comparing the trends in elasticities during the two sub-periods.

Strictly speaking, comparison of values of elasticities measures, indicates different pattern. The values of elasticities of disbursement with respective PRC is higher (1.01) in pre-reform period than its value (0.93) in post-reform period for linear form, while, in the case of the log-linear form, the same elasticity is less (0.92) in the pre-reform period than its value (1.92) in the post-reform period. Exactly opposite trends in elasticities of Disbursements with respective INTC are observed in each case of linear and log-linear forms.

Table 6.16 : Elasticity of Disbursements

	With respect Principal Recovery (PRC)	With respect Interest Amount Collected (INTC)
A. Linear Functional form		
Pre-Reform Period	1.01015*	0.9019*
Post-Reform Period	0.9329*	1.3100
Combined Period	1.0125*	1.2451*
B. Log linear		
Pre-Reform Period	0.9200*	1.091*
Post-Reform Period	1.294*	0.655*
Combined Period	0.748*	0.846*

As far as the combined period is concerned, both the elasticities of disbursements with respect to PRC and INTC derived from the linear form are just higher than unity (1.01 and 1.25 respectively) while, both these elasticities are inelastic (0.75 and 0.85 respectively) in the case of log-linear form. In the combined period, the impact of Interest Amount Collected on Disbursement (in terms of marginal values and elasticities) are higher than the impact of Principle Recovery on Disbursements made by Andhra Pradesh State Financial Corporation.

So far, separate influences of PRC and INTC on Disbursement are investigated from two variable regressions. The results explain significant impact of these variables on Disbursement. Accordingly one more attempt is made to run three variable regression (Disbursement is regressed on both PRC and INTC as independent variable in the same functional form). However, collinearity between PRC and INTC effected the OLS results. It means that one of the regression coefficient of either INTC or PRC resulted in insignificant t-ratios. The results of three variable model are presented in the Appendix Tables 6.a and 6.b.

Profits of the Corporation Before Tax

The APSFC is not a profit motive organisation. The SFCs have been specifically set up for the purpose of helping the business concerns of small and medium units.

Table 6.17 Profits of the APSFC During Pre and Post-Reform Period

(Rs. In lakhs)

Pre-Reform Period year	Profits before tax	Post-Reform period year	Profits before tax
1976-77	93.52	1991-92	302.19
1977-78	126.08	1992-93	606.31
1978-79	5.27	1993-94	1691.65
1979-80	80.47	1994-95	1530.74
1980-81	191.22	1995-96	216
1981-82	345.54	1996-97	301.12
1982-83	453.48	1997-98	104.17
1983-84	493.88	1998-99	141.96
1984-85	551.25	1999-00	247.28
1985-86	546.91	2001-01	268.08
1986-87	307.04	2001-02	113.76
1987-88	443.25	2002-03	369.19
1988-89	454.21	2003-04	601.44
1989-90	790.04	2004-05	690.96
1990-91	415.72	2005-06	783.63
Total	**5297.88**	**Total**	**7968.48**

Source: Various Annual Reports of APSFC.

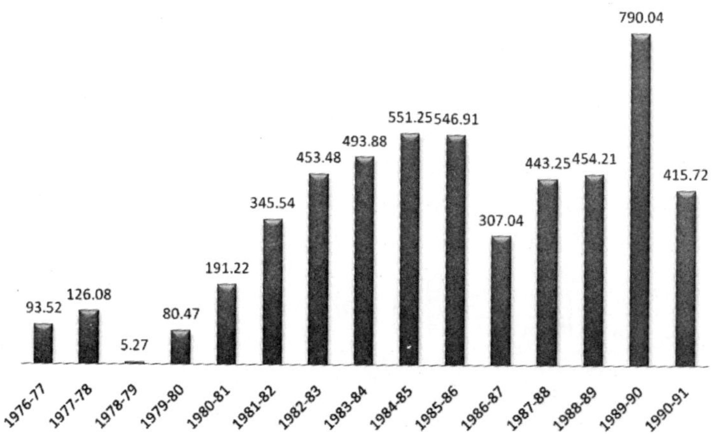

Diagram 5.5 : Profits of the Corporation During the Pre-Reform Period

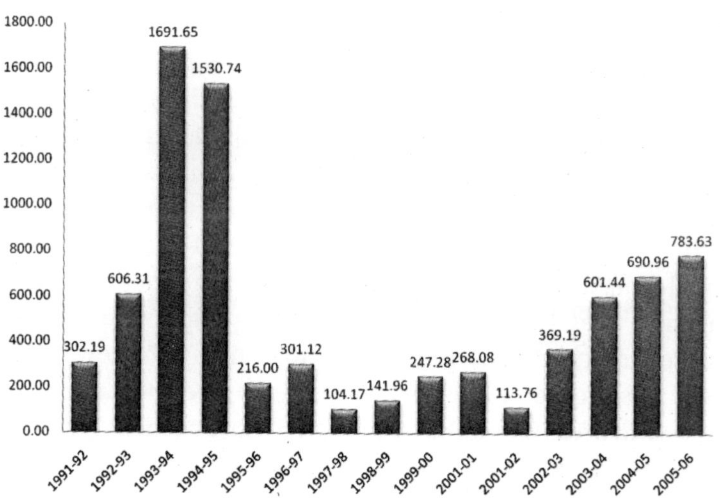

Diagram 5.6 : Profits of the Corporation During the Post-Reform Period

The profits of the Corporation during the pre-reform period are shown in Table 5.17. As can be seen from the table, the profits before tax increased from Rs. 93.52 lakhs to Rs. 415.72 lakhs during the pre-reform period. The total profit of the Corporation amounted to Rs. 5297.88 lakhs during pre-reform period. The Corporation earned high profits during the post-reform period. In this period the profits varies between 104.17 lakhs and Rs. 1691.65. The Corporation earned high amount of profit during the year 1993-94, while lesser profits are registered in the year 1997-98 with the amount Rs. 104.17 lakhs. The total amount of the Corporation during the post-reform period stood at Rs. 7968.48 lakhs. It may be concluded that the profits of the corporation are relatively more impressive during the post-reform period when compared to the pre-reform period. The profits of corporation during pre-reform period and post-reform period are shown in Diagrams 5.5 and 5.6 respectively.

Rate of Interest of the Corporation

The statistical information relating to the rates of interest of the corporation to different categories and different types of schemes for the year 1990-91 and 2005-06 are shown in Tables 5.18 and 5.19. A glance at these two tables reveals that the rate of interest of the Corporation has been slightly reduced in 2005-06 when compared to 1990-91 in respect of small scale industries and medium scale industries. It may be inferred that the APSFC has been playing a vital role as purveyor financial assistance. Comparatively the lower rate of interest in the year 2005-06 is also excepted to promote the backward areas as well as other than backward areas resulting in balanced industrial development, which is one of avowed objective of the Corporation. It also interesting to note from the table that the relatively lower rates of interest extended to transport sector in 2005-06 is welcoming feature in process of infrastructure development of the country.

Table 5.18 : Rate of Interest of the Corporation 1990-91

Sl.No	Category	Net Rate per annum%
1.	Small Scale Industries:	
	1. In notified Backward districts:	
	a. for loans sanctioned up to Rs. 1.00 lakh	12.00
	b. for loans sanctioned above Rs. 1.00 lakh	12.50
	2. In other than Backward areas:	
	a. Up to an extent of Rs. 25.00 lakhs	13.50
	b. Over and above Rs. 25.00 lakhs and up to Rs. 60.00 lakhs	14.00
2.	Medium Scale Industries/Nursing Homes/Hotels/Electro Medical Equipment Scheme:	
	1. In notified Backward areas	12.50
	2. Other than Backward areas	14.00
3.	Single Window Scheme:	
	a. Term Loan on fixed assets	
	- notified backward areas:	
	(i) for loans sanctioned up to Rs. 1 lakh	12.00
	(ii) for loans sanctioned above Rs. 1 lakh	12.50
	- in other than notified backward areas	13.50
	b. Loan towards working capital	
	- if the w/c loan is up to Rs. 2.00 lakhs	14.00
	- if the w/c loan is above Rs. 2.00 lakhs But not exceeding Rs. 2.50 lakhs	15.50
4.	Transport Loans:	
	1. up to 2 vehicles	12.50
	2. More than 2, but up to 6 vehicles	15.00
	3. for Ex-servicemen	12.50

Source: Annual Report of APSFC 1990-91.

Table 5.19 : Rate of Interest of the Corporation 2005-06

Sl.No.	Type of Scheme and Loan Amount	Net Rate per annum%
1.	Term Loans to Tiny and SSI sector including Composite Loans	
	i) Up to Rs. 50,000	10.00
	ii) Above Rs. 50,000 and up to Rs. 2.00 lakh	10.50
	iii) Above Rs. 2.00 lakh and up to Rs. 25.00 lakh	10.50
	iv) Above Rs. 25.00 lakh	10.75
2.	Transport Loans:	
	i) Up to Rs. 50,000	10.00
	ii) Above Rs. 50,000 and up to Rs. 2.00 lakh	10.50
	iii) Above Rs. 2.00 lakh and up to Rs. 25.00 lakh	10.50
	iv) Above Rs. 25.00 lakh	10.75
3.	All Working Capital Term Loans /Working Capital Loans sanctioned	
	Under Single Window Scheme/Working Capital Loans to Civil Contractors.	13.00
4.	Term Loans to MSI/(Non-SSI Sector)	13.00

Source: Annual Reports of APSFC 2005-06

During the post-reform period the Corporation has been colleting relatively more Interest from the self employed schemes which should be reduced due to prevailing unemployment conditions in the State.

Thus, a spectacular performance of the Corporation is noticeable in terms of sanctions and disbursements besides making profits. This will have a significant influence on the sustained growth of industries and subsequent development of the economy. On the recovery front also, the Corporation has registered an impressive performance by achieving the highest ever recovery. Though the rate of interest charged by APSFC was quite higher in pre-reform period, it is drastically reduced to around 10 per cent to accelerate industrial development in the state of Andhra Pradesh. Hence, the rate of interest charged by the Corporation, and response of the borrowers in the repayment of loans augurs well for the future development of the State.

The reduction in the interest rates will be also useful to encourage and attract the unemployed professionals and particularly the first generation entrepreneurs of weaker sections and minority communities in the society. As such, the Corporation has to maintain a reasonable level of rate of interest. In this context, the next chapter would be concentrated on employment generation of schemes and the first generation entrepreneurs belonging to the weaker sections of the society assisted by the APSFC.

CHAPTER

6

APSFC's Scheme-wise Analysis

Introduction

In order to achieve its objectives, APSFC has been promoting innovative schemes keeping in view the changing needs of entrepreneurs to cater to various industrial and market segments. It has also launched special schemes for women entrepreneurs and for first generation entrepreneurs belonging to weaker sections of the society. The Corporation has supported the Government's Industrial Investment Policies by introducing specific schemes for the educated unemployed under 'Crash Programme' and 'Self-Employment Scheme for Young Entrepreneurs'. It operates many schemes for modernization and up gradation of technology.

The objective of this chapter is to throw light on various schemes assisted by the APSFC in Section I and to analyse the scheme-wise classification of sanctions, disbursements, value of out put and employment generation in Section II. In Section III, an attempt is made to analyse the APSFC's assistance to weaker sections of the society so as to examine their 'financial inclusion'. This analysis is confined to an in depth study of the post-reform period only.

SECTION I

The various schemes assisted by the APSFC are discussed below.

General Loans

The General Loans Scheme was introduced in order to help existing and new tiny, small, medium scale units and service sector enterprises. This loan meets a part of cost of land, building, plant, machinery and other fixed assets. The loan is considered at 75 per cent on eligible assets.

Hotels Scheme

Under this scheme, the Corporation sanctions loans for setting up hotels, motels, restaurant projects, for construction of single star, two star and three star hotels with modern facilities. The Schemes are considered by APSFC after getting the approvals from Dept of Tourism, Government of AP/ Government of India, and the approvals from municipal authorities after satisfying the minimum standards fixed by state and Central Governments. The scheme also provides loans for setting up bars and restaurants, for purchase of land, construction of civil works, purchase of kitchen equipment, crockery, air conditioners, DG sets, music system, furniture, interiors etc. The units, which are in operation for a minimum period of three years, are considered for these loans.

Scheme for Tourism Related Facilities

In order to develop tourism related facilities, the Corporation has been also sanctioning loans for development of amusement parks, cultural centers, conventional centers, restaurants, travel, transport and tourism service agencies etc. The cost of these projects, however, should not exceed Rs. 20 cores and there should be approvals from tourism development agencies.

Assistance to Hospitals/Nursing Homes

The financial assistance is also extended for setting up of allopathic nursing homes and hospitals, having not only qualified P.G. doctors on full time basis but also having a minimum strength of 10 beds. The cost of projects should not exceed Rs. 20 Crores and there should be approved municipal plan with a minimum land of 300 sq. yards.

Assistance for Acquiring Electro Medical Equipment

This scheme provides for qualified medical practitioners including ayurvedic doctors, and the facility to acquire electro-medical and other related equipments. Entrepreneurs other than qualified practitioners are also eligible under this scheme. The eligibility allows 75 per cent cost of the electro-medical equipment.

Assistance for Setting up of Industrial Estates

This scheme gives assistance for development of Industrial Estates. The minimum land provided is 10 acres. The project's proposals should include construction of sheds. The assistance could be used for purchase of land, cost of land development, cost of stamp duty etc., besides the development of industrial facilities such as approach roads, drainage, water supply system, power distribution lines, central effluent treatment plant, multi-stored industrial buildings etc. The total cost of project does not exceed Rs.12 crores.

Single Window Scheme

Under this scheme the Corporation sanctions loans to extremely deserving units with venture outlay not exceeding Rs. 2 crores including the working capital requirement and for acquiring fixed assets. The repayment period is 8 years and three years in the case of term loans and working capital term loans respectively.

Road Laying work under build Operate Transport Scheme

This scheme provides assistance to "A" class civil contractors of reputed construction companies, who are ready to work in the construction of roads and buildings. The project cost is based on collateral security. The repayment period is three years.

Scheme for Qualified Professionals

This scheme facilitates to provide assistance to qualified professionals in the fields of management such as accountancy, medicine, engineering etc. Entrepreneurs can use the assistance for setting up of their own professional practice, consultancy venture and for acquiring additional equipments. However, the cost of land and building, should not exceed 50 per cent of total project cost. The total cost of project should not exceed Rs. 20 lakhs.

Mahila Udyam Nidhi Scheme

All industrial projects promoted by women with minimum of 51 per cent share in equity are covered under this scheme. The service activities like hospitals, nursing homes, hotels etc., run by Mahila Udyam are also covered under this scheme. It mainly emphasises on the new units, expansion, modernization, and technology up gradation. The project cost should not exceed Rs. 10 lakhs.

National Equity Fund Scheme

To strengthen the project in tiny and small scale sectors irrespective of location the Corporation has been giving assistance not only to new units but also for existing projects to meet the outlay on modernization and expansion. The minimum promoter's contribution is 10 per cent of the fixed assets. The project cost is subject to a maximum of Rs. 10 lakhs, with five per cent service charge and with Debt Equity ratio of 1.857.

Super Entrepreneur's Scheme

This scheme has been started for the entrepreneurs already existing for seven years of which five years shall be associated with the Corporation. The entrepreneurs who have already repaid 75 per cent of the original term loan availed, are qualified for the scheme. The existing entrepreneurs with 26 percent or more stake and holding not less than 51 per cent stake in the new unit are also eligible. The scheme facilitates for acquiring fixed assets required for expansion, modernization, diversification, and parts of other equipment.

The minimum limit for sanction is Rs. 5.00 lakhs. The minimum promoter's contribution is 22.50 per cent and 25 per cent in the case of Small Scale Industries (SSIs) and Medium Scale Industries (MSI) respectively. The total debt equity ratio is 2 : 1 and the interest concession is 0.5 per cent for prompt repayment.

General Entrepreneur++ Scheme (GES ++)

The Corporation has designed a General Entrepreneur++ Scheme for existing units in operation at least for 5 years of which three years shall be associated with the Corporation. The unit should have repaid at least 50 per cent of term loan availed. The existing entrepreneurs with 26 per cent or more stake and holding not less than 51 per cent of the stake in the new unit are also eligible. The minimum promoter's contribution is 22.5 per cent and 25 percent in the case of SSI's and MSI's respectively. The debt equity ratio is 2:1 while the interest rate concession is 0.30 per cent and extra interest concession of 0.5 per cent for prompt repayment in the last 3 years.

General Entrepreneurs Scheme A+ (GES A+)

The General Entrepreneurs Scheme A+ is designed to promote units after completion of one year from the date of moratorium period subject to a minimum period of three years association with the Corporation. The existing good entrepreneurs with

26 per cent or more stake and holding not less than 51 per cent of stake in the new units are also eligible.

Senior Successful Entrepreneur Scheme

For outstanding entrepreneurs in existence for a minimum period of 7 years and who have not availed financial assistance from the Corporation and earning net profits come under this category. However, the overall debt equity ratio should not exceeding 2 : 1 ratio.

Scheme for Acquisition of ISC 9000 Series Certificates by SSI Units

Existing industrial concerns in the SSI sector having a good record of past performance and sound financial position which:

(*i*) have been in operation for at least four years;

(*ii*) have earned profit and declared dividends during the preceding two financial years;

(*iii*) have not been in the default list of banks; and

(*iv*) have been exporting their products directly or indirectly or have plans to manufacture products for exports, are eligible for acquisition of ISC 9000 Series Certificates.

Marketing Assistance Scheme for SSI Products

The Corporation has designed this scheme for individuals, partnership firms, private and public limited companies to enrich their skills in marketing small and village industry products. The financial assistance is given for marketing related activities, and for setting up of new showrooms, renovation of existing showrooms within the country or abroad. The development of infrastructural projects, for providing marketing support to SSI units, and any other activity directed towards promoting the marketing of SSI products are taken care of under this scheme. The assistance is also extended to land, buildings, storage bins, interiors, equipment, furniture and working capital term loans.

Working Capital Term Loan

The working capital term loans are provided to meet the additional working capital requirements of the existing profit making units in operation for minimum period of two or three years, with a net profit for two years and cash profit for 1 year. More over, the units should be regular in making repayments to the Corporation and they should have paid at least 25 per cent of the original term loans availed. The overall debt equity ratio should not be more than 2:1 for the working capital term loans of above Rs. 5 lakhs.

Self-employment for the Ex-servicemen

The social responsibility of the society is to rehabilitate the ex-servicemen as well as their widows, who have dedicated their lives for preservation of the freedom of our country. In order to fulfil this noble objective, the Corporation has started operating this scheme in association with Director of Sainic Board. Under this scheme the assistance is given for setting up industries, hostels, tourism related activities, gas tankers, tippers and payloads for which seed capital is not available. However, in case of transport vehicles, and the project cost should not exceed Rs. 15 lakhs, while the minimum promoter's contribution is 10 per cent of the project cost.

Term Loan to Practicing Doctors

The Corporation introduced term loans to practicing doctors with minimum qualification of MBBS, BAM/BHMS, BDS/MDS/DHMMS and to physiotherapy unit holders who are paying income tax for the last two financial years. Assistance is provided for setting up of additional fixed assets like furniture, computers, office automation system, ambulance, car or van, acquiring site, interiors decoration, renovation of the premises etc. A minimum amount of Rs. 3 lakhs and a maximum amount of Rs. 25 lakhs for MBBS, BDS, MDS, BAMS, BHMS, Physiotherapy and Rs. 5 lakhs for DHMS doctors are given. The debt equity ratio is 3:1 for loans up to Rs. 10 lakhs and 2:1 for loans above Rs. 10 lakhs.

Credit Linked Capital Subsidy Scheme for Technology Upgradation of SSI Units

In order to assist the existing SSI units going in for technology up gradation in the specified products, 15 percent capital subsidy on loan amount is available under this scheme.

Super Bazar or Retail out lets Scheme for Marketing of SSI Products and others

This scheme is intended to benefit the existing SSI units, individuals, partnership concerns, private and public limited companies having a good track record and sound financial position. The main emphasis of this scheme is to acquire land, building, show room facilities, office equipment, core working capital etc. A minimum financial assistance of Rs. 10 lakhs, and a maximum amount of Rs. 1 crore is given with debt equity ratio of 2 : 1 and the repayment period is five years with one year moratorium.

Scheme for Export-oriented Units

The small sector units with a good track record and sound financial position which are exporting 75 per cent of their production in a year are eligible for assistance under this scheme. New units would be considered for market tie-up for exporting their products. Assistance under this scheme may be availed for setting up industrial units or service units engaged in exporting. Minimum financial assistance is up to Rs. 25 lakhs with debt equity ratio of 2:1, while the repayment period is seven years with a moratorium up to one year.

Working Capital Term Loan for Seasonal Industries

The Corporation has designed this scheme for seasonal industries. The existing profit making units in operation for a minimum period of two to three years with a net profit for two years and cash profit for one year are eligible. The unit should be regular in making repayment to the Corporation and should have paid at least 25 per cent of the original loan availed. There should not be any accumulated cash losses. The Corporation sanctions loans ranging between Rs. 5 lakhs to Rs. 1 crore under this scheme.

Scheme for Establishment, Expansion and Modernization/Technology Upgradation of Food Processing Industries and other Related Industries

This scheme is launched by the Corporation to provide financial assistance for food processing industries and others in connection with modernization, technology up gradation. This also includes ancillary units. In order to be qualified, the Units shall be in operation at least for a period of three years. This scheme applies to units engaged in exporting processed foods in horticulture, agriculture, animal husbandry, fishery, agro-food processing industries and allied industries for purchase of capital equipment, need based civil works, acquisition of land, technical know–how, improvement in packing etc., The debt equity ratio is 2:1, while the repayment period for expansion of existing units is 5 years and 8 years in the case of others with a moratorium period of one year.

Scheme for Financial Assistance for Setting up Private Market Yards

The Corporation has designed scheme for purchase of land, construction of civil works such as sale-halls, action plat forms, shops cum godowns, in connection with market yards. In addition to this, assistance is given to supplementary civil works such as water supply connections and weigh bridges, cleaning and drying equipments etc. The minimum loan under this scheme is Rs. 25 lakhs and the maximum loan eligibility is 75 per cent on the eligible fixed assets including land. The maximum repayment period is 8 years with a moratorium period up to two years.

Scheme for Financial Assistance to SC/ST Entrepreneurs for Setting up of Industrial Units and Service Enterprises

Under this scheme, the Corporation extends financial assistance to Scheduled Caste/Schedule Tribe entrepreneurs for construction of civil works and acquiring the equipment and machinery or any other items required by the industrial units and also to service enterprises. The minimum amount of term loan is Rs. 5 lakhs. The loan eligibility is up to 75 per cent on the eligible components of the projects. This scheme also provides seed capital assistance. The eligible borrowers under the category of the SC/ST entrepreneurs, who are also the chief promoters, shall have at least 25 per cent of share holding and with close relatives belonging to this category put together shall hold at least 51 per cent of the equity capital proposed in the scheme. Repayment period is eight years in case of term loans with a moratorium up to two years.

Scheme for Financial Assistance to Women Entrepreneurs for Setting up of Industrial Units and Service Enterprises

The Corporation has also introduced schemes to encourage women entrepreneurs to set up industrial ventures in small scale sector. Special development programmes were conducted at various places in the districts by the industrial promotional agencies in which the corporation actively participated to assist women entrepreneurs. Under this scheme, the women promoters shall have at least 51 per cent of the equity capital proposed in the scheme. The loan will be repayable over eight years with a moratorium up to two years.

SECTION-II

The scheme-wise classification of sanctions, disbursements, value of out put and employment generation is analyzed in this section.

Scheme-wise Classification of Sanctions Made by APSFC During 1990-91 to 2005-06

The Corporation extends financial assistance for a variety of schemes. In this section an attempt is made to analyse the most important schemes of the Corporation which are detailed in Table 6.1. On the basis of the assistance of loans sanctioned by the Corporation during 1990-91 to 2005-06, schemes are arranged in the ranking order. Of the various schemes that come under the category of sanctions, the general loan scheme occupies the first position by claiming a total amount of Rs. 11239.98 crores constituting 39.22 per cent of the total sanctions made during 1990-91 to 2005-06. These sanctions extending to 2459 units have resulted in generating a value of out put of Rs. 6642,33,58 crores and employment generation of 164,145 numbers. The short term finance assistance takes second position, which received a total amount of Rs. 5314.97 crores covering 2485 units. It has created 2485 employment opportunities along with a value of output accounting for Rs. 1601.17 crores. The short term finance scheme is followed by 'Assistance to Tourism Facility', which obtained Rs. 4475.86 crores to 957 units. The employment generation in this scheme is quite significant numbering 23605 with an output value of Rs. 3548.26 crores. It is evident from the table that GESA++ has claimed Rs. 1958.59 crores extending to 154 units. The employment generated by this scheme stood at 12,762. The value of out put generated under this scheme works out to be Rs. 13336.24 crores. The next important scheme is 'Hotel/

Table 6.1 : Scheme-wise Sanctions Made by the Corporation During 1991-92 to 2005-06

(Amount in Rs. 000)\

Schemes of Assistance	Sanctions	% to Total	Number generation	Employment	Value of output
General Loans Scheme	11239982	32.99	2459	164145	66423358
Short-term Finance Schemes	5314971	15.60	2485	18114	16011740
Assistance for Tourism Facility	4475863	13.14	957	23605	35482603
GESA++	1958591	5.75	154	12762	13336240
Hotel /Motels Restaurant Scheme	1865100	5.47	394	9942	1913033
GES A	1777502	5.22	543	10447	3220611
National Equity Fund Scheme	1561111	4.58	641	73530	1561556
Assistance to Practicing Doctors	1111636	3.26	737	7776	1173031
Transport Scheme	1102309	3.24	3074	101989	1459758
Scheme for Acquiring Bore wells drilling	643999	1.89	453	26495	2031476
Single Window scheme	640344	1.88	2795	6903	1992179
GES A+	548656	1.61	50	3024	6788967
Scheme for Qualified Professionals	518957	1.52	136	1809	2903340
Mahila Udyam Nidhi Scheme	322954	0.95	425	1936	461704
Quality Control Scheme	284486	0.83	600	1200	193071
Equipment Refinance	195643	0.57	139	165625	942340
Scheme of Assistance for DG sets	143275	0.42	339	960	232122
Composite loans	90859	0.27	3039	793	148364
Modernization Scheme	76766	0.23	57	12576	284421
Rehabilitation Schemes	48033	0.14	32	845	28054
100% Export-oriented units Scheme	43601	0.13	11	220	174404
Self-employment Scheme	34039	0.10	306	45	4732
Ex-Serviceman Scheme	33473	0.10	83	379	44252
Bill Discounting Scheme	15000	0.04	1	81	14000
Assistance for Purchase of Mobile Van	12824	0.04	5	57	99270
Composite loans-SES	8423	0.02	322	2269	145700
Scheme for Physical Handicapped	1722	0.01	15	3748	14
Manufacturing Installation					
Renewable Scheme	1315	0.00	2	127	125000
Relief Assistance to Natural Calamities	621	0.00	3	0	0
Total	**34072055**		**20257**	**651402**	**157195340**

Source: APSFC Annual Reports

Motels/Restaurant Scheme', which accounts for Rs. 1,86,51 crores to 394 units. It has created employment and value of out put of 9942 number and Rs. 1913.03 crores respectively. The "National Equity Fund Scheme" received an amount of Rs. 1561.11 crores extending over 641 units. This scheme has generated 73,530 jobs while the value of out put of the covered units is Rs. 1561.55 crores. In the case of Assistance to Practicing Doctors, the data reveals that the Corporation has sanctioned Rs. 1111.63 crores to 737 doctors during the study period. As such this scheme has generated 7776 jobs along with a value of services accounting for Rs. 1173.03 crores. The next place goes to Transport Scheme for which the total sanctions stood at Rs. 1102.30 crores, assisting a total of 3074 units. Both the employment generated and value of output in this scheme are quite significant. This scheme has created 1,01,989 jobs and Rs. 1459.75 crores value of out put. The Transport Scheme is followed by "Bore Well Drilling Scheme". Totally this scheme claimed Rs. 643.99 crores covering 453 units. This scheme has created 26,495 jobs and Rs. 203.1476 crores of value of out put. Next, comes the 'single window scheme,' which has claimed Rs. 6403.44 crores covering a number of 2795 units. It has generated employment numbering 6903. The value of out put of this scheme is Rs. 1992.17 crores. The GES A+ scheme follows next, obtaining Rs. 548.65 crores spreading over 161 units, providing around 50 jobs and creating a value of output around Rs. 6788.96 crores. The Scheme for Qualified Professional's obtained from the Corporation an amount of Rs. 518.95 crores in the form of sanctions assisting to 136 units. This scheme has created 1809 jobs. An output value of 2903.34 crores has been generated under this scheme. 'Mahila Udyam Nidhi Scheme', comes next in obtaining sanctions and it has accounted for Rs. 322.95 crores and covered 425 units. This scheme has generated 1936 jobs and created Rs. 461.70 crores value of output. Quality Control Scheme could claim Rs. 284.48 crores, numbering 600 units. This scheme has created 1200 jobs and a value of out of Rs. 193.07 crores.

It is also observed from Table 6.1 that the Corporation has sanctioned only a fewer amounts to schemes such as Relief Assistance Calamities Scheme, Manufacturing Renewable Scheme, Scheme for Physically Handicapped, Composite Loan Scheme, Assistance for Purchase of Mobile Van, Bill Discounting Scheme, Ex-service Men Scheme, Self Employment Scheme, the Scheme for 100 per cent export oriented units and Rehabilitation Scheme.

Relief Assistance for Natural Calamities is given to only three units with a total sanctioned amount of Rs. 0.621crores. Manufacturing of Renewable Scheme accounted for Rs. 1.31 crores covering two units only. The employment generation, and value of output are also not impressive. It is particularly distressing to note that the Scheme for Physically Handicapped could get Rs. 17.22 crores by way of sanctioning covering 15 units, and providing 3748 jobs. Composite Loans Sanction stood at Rs. 8.42 lakhs covering 322 units. This scheme has generated 2269 jobs and a value of output of Rs. 145.7 crores. 'Composite Loans Scheme' is followed by Assistance for Purchase of Mobile Van accounted for Rs. 12.82 crores covering 5 units with 57 jobs and it has generated Rs. 99.27 crores value of output. In the case of Ex-servicemen Scheme the total sanctions amounted to Rs. 33.47 crores, assisting to 83 units with 379 jobs and a value of output of Rs. 44.25 crores. The Self-employment Scheme accounted for Rs. 34.03 crores extending to 306 units, and providing 45 jobs with an output value of Rs. 4.73 crores.

It may be inferred from this table, that the APSFC is playing a magnificent role, in providing assistance by way of sanctions to different schemes.

Scheme-wise Classification of Disbursements made by APSF During 1990-91 to 2005-06

The information relating to scheme-wise disbursements is shown in Table 6.2 and the following observations are made from the Table. It is clear from the table that in terms of disbursements also the general loans schemes occupied the first position by getting total amount of Rs. 6875.67 crores consisting of 28.06 percent in total disbursements during 1990-91 to 2005-06. Similarly, the short term finance also occupied second position which received a total amount of Rs. 5025.45 crores, constituting 20.51 per cent of the total disbursements. This is followed by "Assistance Tourism Facility" which obtained Rs. 3539.53 crores, claiming 14.45 per cent. Assistance Tourism Facility scheme is followed by GES++. This scheme received 6.35 per cent of the total disbursements. The next place goes to GES A scheme, which has claimed Rs. 1440.83 crores accounting for 5.88 per cent of the total disbursements. In the case of Transport Schemes to proportion of disbursements is 4.30 per cent. While the schemes relating to Assistance to Practicing Doctors Schemes claimed 4 per cent of the total disbursements, the Hotel/Motel/Restaurant Schemes have received 2.93 per cent of the disbursements. Similarly, the schemes for Bore Well Drilling obtained 2.42 per cent of the disbursements, while the single window scheme and the scheme for professionals obtained 1.92 per cent and 1.84 per cent respectively. The National Equity Fund Scheme and the GES A+ scheme could get 1.75 per cent and 1.42 per cent of the disbursements. As can be seen from the table, the remaining schemes could get only less than one per cent of the total disbursements.

It is distressing to note that, Bill Discounting Scheme and more particularly the Relief Assistance to Natural Calamities Scheme, and the Scheme for Physical Handicapped, did not get a better share in the total disbursements. In addition to this, the Composite Loans, and Manufacturing and Renewable Scheme, Assistance for Purchase of Mobile Van, and "the 100 per cent export oriented units" have been claiming lesser than one per cent of the total disbursements in the same period.

Form this analysis, it may be observed that the sanctions made and disbursements effected are more or less similar with respective the units-wise schemes under the study. From

Table 6.2 : Scheme-wise DisbursementsMade by the Corporation During 1991-92 to 2005-06

(Amount in Rs. 000

Schemes of Assistance	Disbursements	% to Total
General Loans Scheme	6875673	28.06
Short-term Finance Schemes	5025459	20.51
Assistance for Tourism Facility	3539536	14.45
GESA++	1555246	6.35
GES A	1440883	5.88
Transport Scheme	1053607	4.30
Assistance to Practicing Doctors	979643	4.00
Hotel /Motels Restaurant Scheme	716855	2.93
Scheme for Acquiring Bore wells drilling	592894	2.42
Single Window scheme	470723	1.92
Scheme for Qualified Professionals	450709	1.84
National Equity Fund Scheme	428582	1.75
GES A+	348197	1.42
Mahila Udyam Nidhi Scheme	196944	0.80
Quality Control Scheme	196353	0.80
Equipment Refinance	147372	0.60
Self-employment Scheme	131393	0.54
Scheme of Assistance for DG sets	104069	0.42
Composite loans	79638	0.33
Modernization Scheme	52260	0.21
Rehabilitation Schemes	43880	0.81
Ex-Serviceman Scheme	25911	0.11
100% Export Oriented units Scheme	19572	0.08
Assistance for Purchase of Mobile Van	12392	0.05
Bill Discounting Scheme	6196	0.03
Manufacturing Installation Renewable Scheme	5424	0.02
Composite loans-SES	2875	0.01
Scheme for Physical Handicapped	709	0.00
Relief Assistance to Natural Calamities	0	0.00
Total	**24502995**	**100.00**

Source: APSFC Annual Reports.

this analysis, it is also inferred that in the case of employment, the schemes such as Equipment Refinance Scheme, General Loans Scheme, Transport Loan Scheme, National Equity Funds Scheme, Scheme for Acquiring Bore Well, Assistance for Tourism Facility, Short Term Finance, GES A++, Modernization Scheme, GES A, Hotel/Motel/Restaurants Assistance to Practicing Doctors, Single Window Scheme and Physically Handicapped Schemes are found to be quite impressive in generation of employment.

However, the Relief Assistance for Natural Calamities, Self Employment Scheme, Assistance for Purchase of Mobile Sales Vans for marketing support, Bill Discounting Scheme, Manufacturing, Installation of Renewable energy saving system, the 100% export oriented units, Ex-service Men Scheme, Composite Loans, Rehabilitation Scheme, Scheme of Assistance for DG sets, could not provide larger number of jobs.

The analysis relating to value of output revealed that General Loans, Assistance for Tourism Facility, Short Term Finance, GES A++, GES A+, GES A, Scheme for Qualified Professionals Scheme, Acquiring for bore wells, Single Window Scheme, Hotel/Motel/Restaurants Scheme, National Equity Funds Scheme, Transport Scheme have been creating spectacular value of output to the state economy. On the other hand schemes such as Relief Assistance for Natural Calamities, Scheme for Physically Handicapped, Self Employment Scheme, Bill Discounting Scheme, and Manufacturing/Installation of renewable scheme, Rehabilitation Scheme, Ex-service Men Scheme, have been accounting for lesser value of output to the state economy.

Thus, it is heartening to note that the Corporation has been not only starting new schemes but also updating the entrepreneurial needs to suit the requirements of globalization. It is also interesting to note that a good number of schemes have been initiated by the Corporation. From this analysis, it is concluded that the sanctions made and disbursements effected have resulted not only impressive generation of employment and substantial amounts of contribution by value of output to the state economy during the study period.

SECTION III

In this section an attempt is made to analyse the APSFC's assistance to weaker sections of the society so as to examine their 'financial inclusion'. In India the financial institutions witnessed tremendous growth in volume and complexity over the years. Despite making significant improvements in all the areas relating to financial viability, profitability and competitiveness, there were concerns that the financial institutions had not been able to include adequately the vulnerable sections of the society. Due to this financial exclusion, disadvantaged people are lagging behind in the process of economic development. As a result, not only the income disparities are widening but also poverty reduction to the targeted levels has not been achieved. The weaker sections in India mainly consist of Scheduled Castes (SCs), Scheduled Tribes (STs), Other Backward Classes (OBCs) and Minorities. The Other Castes/Communities (OCs) group is considered to be of relatively advanced communities. It has been argued that the fruits of development have not been filtered down to the weaker sections. In order to achieve growth with social justice, economic growth is not only to be accelerated but the growth should be avoiding perpetuation of inequalities. In other words, the economic growth should not result in social exclusion. This necessitates 'inclusive growth'. In this context, it is proposed to examine in this section the efforts made by the Corporation to strengthen the financial inclusion of the poor and the disadvantaged sections.

Number of Sanctions Assisted by the Corporation to weaker Sections During 1991-92 to 2005-06

The data relating to the number of sanctions made by the Corporation to weaker sections during 1991-92 to 2005-06 is shown in Table 6.3. Out of the total number of 1705 sanctions made by the APSFC to SCs, as high as 85.11 per cent are in the form of term loan's. The special loans constituted around 11.85 per cent, while working capital loans constituted only a meager 3.04 percent. Bridge loans did not figure at all.

In respect of STs, the total number of loans sanctioned amounted for 239, out of which as high as 86.19 percent are in form of term loans. The special loans are worked out to be 11.29 per cent, while the working capital loans accounted for 2.52 per cent. There were no sanctioned bridge loans during this period.

The analysis of number of sanctions reveals that out of total number of sanctions, the term loans dominated in the total number of sanctions. Another interesting to note from the table is that the total number of sanctioned loans given to the weaker sections have been reducing during the period under study.

Amount of Sanctions made by the Corporation to Weaker Sections

The data pertaining to amount of sanctions made by the Corporation to weaker sections are presented in the Table 6.4. It is clear from the table, that out of the total sanctioned amount of Rs. 840.22 crores made to SCs, as high as 97.02 per cent went in the form of term loans. More over, the term loans sanctioned reduced from Rs. 107.02 crores in 1991-92 to Rs. 16.05 crores by 2005-06 to SC category. The special loans did not figure from the year 1993-94 to 2005-06 and the total amount in the first two years stood at Rs. 19.21 crores. Bridge loans did not figure in this category.

The table also provides data pertaining to sanctioned amounts to STs. The total amount of sanctions during this

Table 6.3 : Number of Sanctions Given by the Corporation to Weaker Sections During 1991-92 to 2005-06

Years	Scheduled Caste					Scheduled Tribes				
	Term Loans	Working Capital Loans	Special Loans	Bridge Loans	Year-wise Total	Term Loans	Working Capital Loans	Special Loans	Bridge Loans	Year-wise Total
1991-92	522	30	191	0	743	51	2	17	0	70
1992-93	345	15	11	0	371	44	2	6	0	52
1993-94	144	5	0	0	149	17	1	4	0	22
1994-95	64	1	0	0	65	12	1	0	0	13
1995-96	43	1	0	0	44	8	0	0	0	8
1996-97	43	0	0	0	43	8	0	0	0	8
1997-98	33	0	0	0	33	4	0	0	0	4
1998-99	37	0	0	0	37	8	0	0	0	8
1999-00	76	0	0	0	76	18	0	0	0	18
2001-01	53	0	0	0	53	10	0	0	0	10
2001-02	27	0	0	0	27	8	0	0	0	8
2002-03	25	0	0	0	25	6	0	0	0	6
2003-04	17	0	0	0	17	5	0	0	0	5
2004-05	12	0	0	0	12	4	0	0	0	4
2005-06	10	0	0	0	10	3	0	0	0	3
Total	**1451** (85.11)	**52** (3.04)	**202** (11.85)	**0** (0.00)	**1705** (100.00)	**206** (86.19)	**6** (2.52)	**27** (11.29)	**0** (0.00)	**239** (100.00)

Source: APSFC Annual Reports.
The Figures in parentheses indicates percentages to total.

Table 6.4 : Amount of Sanctions Assisted by the Corporation to Weaker Sections During 1991-92 to 2005-06

(Amount in Rs. '000)

	Scheduled Caste					Scheduled Tribes				
Years	Term Loans	Working Capital Loans	Special Loans	Bridge Loans	Year-wise Total	Term Loans	Working Capital Loans	Special Loans	Bridge Loans	Year-wise Total
1991-92	107021	3706	18324	0	129051	13010	102	1819	0	14931
1992-93	71947	1013	894	0	73854	15509	165	1475	0	17149
1993-94	370305	1012	0	0	371317	4306	158	282	0	4746
1994-95	22391	17	0	0	22408	5412	34	0	0	5446
1995-96	20527	59	0	0	20586	4056	0	0	0	4056
1996-97	29696	0	0	0	29696	6553	0	0	0	6553
1997-98	30014	0	0	0	30014	2456	0	0	0	2456
1998-99	26638	0	0	0	26638	163308	0	0	0	163308
1999-00	7952	0	0	0	7952	28402	0	0	0	28402
2001-01	41985	0	0	0	41985	17824	0	0	0	17824
2001-02	18941	0	0	0	18941	6532	0	0	0	6532
2002-03	3933	0	0	0	3933	6145	0	0	0	6145
2003-04	22676	0	0	0	22676	4210	0	0	0	4210
2004-05	25122	0	0	0	25122	3505	0	0	0	3505
2005-06	16054	0	0	0	16054	3370	0	0	0	3370
Total	**815202** (97.02)	**5807** (0.69)	**19218** (2.29)	(0.00)	**840227** (100.00)	**284598** (98.60)	**459** (0.16)	**3576** (1.24)	**0** (0.00)	**288633** (100.00)

Source: APSFC Annual Reports

The figures in parentheses indicates percentages to total

period stood at Rs. 288.63 crores, out of which the term loans accounted for as high of 98.60 per cent. However, the term loans sanctioned during the study period went down from Rs. 13.01 crores to Rs. 3.37 crores. The working capital loans and special loans accounted for 0.16 per cent and 1.24 per cent respectively.

Number of Disbursements made by the Corporation to Weaker Sections During 1991-92 to 2005-06

Table 6.5 provides the statistical information relating to the number of disbursements made by the Corporation during 1991-92 to 2005-06. The total number of loans stood at 1965, out of which 1648 (83.87%) went to term loans, while the working capital loans claimed 3.87 per cent and the special loans obtained 12.26 per cent.

The table also shows the number of disbursements made by the Corporation to STs. The total number of loans recorded is 215, out of which 80 per cent has gone to term loans and 15.35 accounted for special loans, followed by working capital loans which claimed a share of 4.65 per cent in the total.

From the above analysis, it is clear that the term loans dominated both in sanctions made and disbursement effected in respect of both SCs and STs. The special loans, comes next to term loans followed by working capital loans in respect of both sanctions and disbursements. However, it is disheartening to note that in the case of number of disbursements also, the assistance made under different categories of loans to both SCs and STs has been declining during the study period.

Amount of Disbursements made by the Corporation to Weaker Sections During 1991-92 to 2005-06

Table 6.6 presents the amount of disbursements made by the Corporation to SCs. Out of the total disbursements effected to SCs, 87.70 per cent went in the from of term loans. However, the term loans have been reduced from Rs. 88.26

Table 6.5 : Number of Disbursements given by the Corporation to Weaker Sections During 1991-92 to 2005-06

	Scheduled Caste					Scheduled Tribes				
Years	Term Loans	Working Capital Loans	Special Loans	Bridge Loans	Year-wise Total	Term Loans	Working Capital Loans	Special Loans	Bridge Loans	Year-wise Total
1991-92	529	44	204	0	777	49	3	22	0	74
1992-93	326	22	37	0	385	31	5	7	0	43
1993-94	194	5	0	0	199	12	1	2	0	15
1994-95	99	2	0	0	101	6	1	2	0	9
1995-96	22	3	0	0	25	9	0	0	0	9
1996-97	239	0	0	0	239	4	0	0	0	4
1997-98	17	0	0	0	17	3	0	0	0	3
1998-99	29	0	0	0	29	4	0	0	0	4
1999-00	43	0	0	0	43	13	0	0	0	13
2001-01	67	0	0	0	67	16	0	0	0	16
2001-02	21	0	0	0	21	9	0	0	0	9
2002-03	24	0	0	0	24	4	0	0	0	4
2003-04	16	0	0	0	16	5	0	0	0	5
2004-05	11	0	0	0	11	4	0	0	0	4
2005-06	11	0	0	0	11	3	0	0	0	3
Total	**1648** (83.87)	**76** (3.87)	**241** (12.26)	**0** (0.00)	**1965** (100.00)	**172** (80.00)	**10** (4.65)	**33** (15.35)	**0** (0.00)	**215** (100.00)

Source: APSFC Annual Reports.
The figures in parentheses indicates percentages to total.

Table 6.6 : Amount of Disbursements given by the Corporation to Weaker Sections During 1991-92 to 2005-06

(Amount in Rs. '000)

Years	Scheduled Caste					Scheduled Tribes				
	Term Loans	Working Capital Loans	Special Loans	Bridge Loans	Year-wise Total	Term Loans	Working Capital Loans	Special Loans	Bridge Loans	Year-wise Total
1991-92	88268	1879	15262	0	105409	10227	87	1988	0	12302
1992-93	37063	1587	10755	0	49405	9261	331	862	0	10454
1993-94	31978	523	1276	0	33777	3559	68	659	0	4286
1994-95	22345	270	0	0	22615	3673	34	136	0	3843
1995-96	11798	166	0	0	11964	2254	0	0	0	2254
1996-97	16742	0	0	0	16742	3528	0	0	0	3528
1997-98	6640	0	0	0	6640	2522	0	0	0	2522
1998-99	20321	0	0	0	20321	7873	0	0	0	7873
1999-00	32336	0	0	0	32336	22223	0	0	0	22223
2001-01	60903	0	0	0	60903	20552	0	0	0	20552
2001-02	3235	0	0	0	3235	7928	0	0	0	7928
2002-03	33714	0	0	0	33714	2466	0	0	0	2466
2003-04	23901	0	0	0	23901	1758	0	0	0	1758
2004-05	13613	0	0	0	13613	5518	0	0	0	5518
2005-06	21054	3553	13400	0	38007	3370	732	2191	0	6293
Total	**423911** (87.70)	**7978** (1.69)	**40693** (8.61)	**0** (0.00)	**472582** (100.00)	**106712** (93.77)	**1252** (1.10)	**5836** (5.13)	**0** (0.00)	**113800** (100.00)

Source: APSFC Annual Reports.
The figures in parentheses indicates percentages to total.

crores to Rs. 21.05 crores during the study period. The working capital loans have obtained a total amount of Rs. 7.97 lakhs claiming only 1.69 percent. The total amount stood at Rs. 40.69 crores, consisting of 8.61 per cent in the case of special loans. However, during 1994-95 to 2004-05 bridge loans did not figure. 10.22 crores, while it has been reduced to Rs. 3.37 lakhs by 2005-06. The term loans, however, claimed lesser amount of disbursements during 2003-04. While the special loans constituted 5.13 per cent in the total disbursements, the working capital loans accounted for a meager 1.10 per cent during the study period.

Number of Sanctions Extended by the Corporation to Backward Classes (BCs) and other Castes (OCs)

The number of sanctions extended by the Corporation to Backward Classes and Other Castes during 1991-92 to 2005-06 is shown in Table 6.7. The number of term loans with respect to Backward Class is varying between 86 to 1476, and constituted 90.68 per cent in the total loans during the study period. While the working capital loans accounted for 9.27 percent, the special loans constituted only 0.04 per cent for this group. However, the bridge loans could not figure in the total loans. The total number of loans extended to backward classes stood at 4863 during the study period.

Further, the table also provides the number of sanctions made to the other communities. Out of the total number of 20,059 loans, the term loans constituted 94.72 per cent. While the working capital loans accounted for 5.20 per cent, the special loans worked out to be 0.08 per cent. It is observed from the table that the number of working capital loans drastically reduced when compared to term loans during the study period with regard to both backward classes as well as other castes.

Table 6.7 : Number of Sanctions Extended by the Corporation to backward Classes, and other Communities During 1991-92 to 2005-06

	Scheduled Caste					Scheduled Tribes				
Years	Term Loans	Working Capital Loans	Special Loans	Bridge Loans	Year-wise Total	Term Loans	Working Capital Loans	Special Loans	Bridge Loans	Year-wise Total
1991-92	1476	345	2	0	1823	2650	583	10	0	3243
1992-93	1001	59	0	0	1060	1999	251	3	0	2253
1993-94	376	18	0	0	394	912	80	1	0	993
1994-95	174	10	0	0	184	956	38	2	1	997
1995-96	132	10	0	0	142	1134	23	0	0	1157
1996-97	127	2	0	0	129	982	25	0	0	1007
1997-98	121	5	0	0	126	1112	22	0	0	1134
1998-99	131	1	0	0	132	1089	8	0	0	1097
1999-00	159	0	0	0	159	1478	0	0	0	1478
2001-01	155	0	0	0	155	1506	2	0	0	1508
2001-02	137	0	0	0	137	1181	2	0	0	1183
2002-03	135	0	0	0	135	1080	2	0	0	1082
2003-04	108	0	0	0	108	1023	1	0	0	1024
2004-05	86	1	0	0	87	959	5	0	0	964
2005-06	92	0	0	0	92	938	1	0	0	939
Total	**4410** (90.68)	**451** (9.27)	**2** (0.04)	**0** (0.00)	**4863** (100.00)	**18999** (94.72)	**1043** (5.20)	**16** (0.08)	**1** (0.00)	**20059** (100.00)

Source: APSFC Annual Reports.
The figures in parentheses indicates percentages to total.

Sanctions made by the Corporation to Backward Classes (BCs) and other Communities (OCs)

Here an attempt is also made to study the APSFC's sanctions made to backward classes and other castes. Table 6.8 presents the term loans given by the Corporation to BCs. It is clear from the table, in 1991-92 the term loans stood at Rs.187.69 crores and the amount went up to Rs. 215.25 crores. The share of term loans accounted for 98.77 per cent in the total amount sanctioned. Though the working capital loans sanctioned by the Corporation stood at Rs. 16.10 crores in 1991-92, this amount also drastically reduced in the subsequent years. The total sanctioned amount during the study period, however, accounted for Rs. 31.53 crores, comprising 1.21 per cent in the total sanctions. The special loans obtained 0.02 per cent, while the bridge loans did not figure at all.

Further, the table also provides the information relating to other caste category during the same period. In the case of term loans, the sanctioned amount stood at Rs. 1748.27 crores in 1991-92 and it went up to Rs. 4746.40 crores by 2005-06. This constituted 99.56 per cent of the total loan amount sanctioned. The sanctioned amount of working capital loans went down from Rs. 66.98 crores in 1991-92 to 0.89 crores by 2005-06. The amount of loans sanctioned under working capital constituted 0.42 per cent in the total loan amount sanctioned. The special loans and bridge loans accounted each for 0.01 per cent.

Number of Disbursements made by the Corporation to Backward Classes (BCs) and other Castes (OCs)

Table 6.9 provides the number of disbursements extended by the Corporation to Backward Class and Other Communities during 1991-92 to 2005-06. It is clear form the table, that about 5176 number of loans are disbursed to Backward Classes, out of which the term loans claimed 84.49 per cent during the study period. This is followed by working capital loans with 15.46 per cent, while special loans have obtained only 0.06 per cent.

Table 6.8 : Amount ofSanctions Extended by the Corporation to Backward Classes, and other Communities During 1991-92 to 2005-06

(Amount in Rs. '000)

	Scheduled Caste					Scheduled Tribes				
Years	Term Loans	Working Capital Loans	Special Loans	Bridge Loans	Year-wise Total	Term Loans	Working Capital Loans	Special Loans	Bridge Loans	Year-wise Total
1991-92	187699	16107	600	0	204406	1748275	66918	1710	0	1816903
1992-93	221015	7064	0	0	228079	1581496	35537	1150	0	1618183
1993-94	81097	1776	0	0	82873	818012	15075	67	0	833154
1994-95	57928	866	0	0	58794	1311360	8140	210	2000	1321710
1995-96	109917	1942	0	0	111859	1665615	5049	0	0	1670664
1996-97	119945	510	0	0	120455	1365877	8092	0	0	1373969
1997-98	145843	1478	0	0	147321	1846411	6715	0	0	1853126
1998-99	146656	50	0	0	146706	2495119	2275	0	0	2497394
1999-00	206032	0	0	0	206032	3037941	0	0	0	3037941
2001-01	214581	0	0	0	214581	3644714	3750	0	0	3648464
2001-02	220129	0	0	0	220129	3654970	3750	0	0	3658720
2002-03	264624	0	0	0	264624	3538689	3080	0	0	3541769
2003-04	217670	0	0	0	217670	3450136	939	0	0	3451075
2004-05	167557	1740	0	0	169297	3937219	4890	0	0	3942109
2005-06	215252	0	0	0	215252	4746402	897	0	0	4747299
Total	**2575945 (98.77)**	**31533 (1.21)**	**600 (0.02)**	**0 (0.00)**	**2608078 (100.00)**	**38842236 (99.56)**	**165107 (0.42)**	**3137 (0.01)**	**2000 (0.01)**	**39012480 (100.00)**

Source: APSFC Annual Reports.

The figures in parentheses indicates percentages to total.

Table 6.9 : Number of Disbursements Made by the Corporation to Backward Classes, and other Communities During 1991-92 to 2005-06

	Scheduled Caste					Scheduled Tribes				
Years	Term Loans	Working Capital Loans	Special Loans	Bridge Loans	Year-wise Total	Term Loans	Working Capital Loans	Special Loans	Bridge Loans	Year-wise Total
1991-92	1743	248	3	0	1994	2735	595	13	0	3343
1992-93	662	299	0	0	961	1336	347	5	0	1688
1993-94	576	60	0	0	636	890	131	1	0	1022
1994-95	169	15	0	0	184	821	52	1	1	875
1995-96	90	5	0	0	95	897	31	0	0	928
1996-97	89	4	0	0	93	846	12	0	0	858
1997-98	94	1	0	0	95	922	19	0	0	941
1998-99	126	2	0	0	128	942	18	0	0	960
1999-00	145	1	0	0	146	1327	1	0	0	1328
2001-01	157	0	0	0	157	1426	2	0	0	1428
2001-02	117	0	0	0	117	1136	2	0	0	1138
2002-03	133	0	0	0	133	1005	2	0	0	1007
2003-04	98	0	0	0	98	947	1	0	0	948
2004-05	87	1	0	0	88	975	3	0	0	978
2005-06	87	164	0	0	251	855	1	0	0	856
Total	**4373** (84.49)	**800** (15.46)	**3** (0.06)	**0** (0.00)	**5176** (100.00)	**17060** (93.23)	**1217** (6.65)	**20** (0.11)	**1** (0.01)	**18298** (100.00)

Source: APSFC Annual Reports.

The figures in parentheses indicates percentages to total.

Further, the table also provides the information regarding the number of disbursements extended by the Corporation to 'Other Castes'. It reveals that the term loans have obtained a lion's share in the total loans comprising 93.23 per cent, and working capital loans consisting of 6.65 per cent. However, the special loans and bridge loans claimed less than one per cent.

Amount of Disbursements made by the Corporation to Backward Classes (BCs) and other Castes (OCs)

The data relating to amounts disbursed by the Corporation to Backward Class during 1991-92 to 2005-06 are shown in Table 6.10. It is observed from the table, the total amount disbursed by the Corporation to Backward Classes stood at Rs. 3629.12 crores during the study period. Among the four loans, the term loans claimed a major share consisting of 98.61 per cent. On the other hand the working capital loans claimed 1.34 per cent and the special loans 0.05 per cent, while the bridge loans did not figure at all.

Further, the table also shows the amount of disbursements effected by the Corporation to Other Caste/Communities. The Corporation disbursed totally Rs. 29,456.09 crores during the study period. Again the term loans obtained the largest share of disbursements comprising 99.44 per cent of total disbursed amount. The other loans such as working capital loans (0.49%), special loans (0.06%), bridge loans (0.01%) have claimed less than one per cent in the total disbursed amount during the study period. The disbursements made by the Corporation to SCs, STs, BCs, and OCs are shown in diagram 6.1.

The foregoing analysis reveals that out of the total assistance made by the Corporation in terms of sanctions and disbursements to different categories, the category of 'Other Caste' received a major proportion when compared to SCs, STs and OBCs. The loan-wise category analysis reveals that a higher priority is given to term loans rather than other

Table 6.10 : Number of Disbursements Extended by the Corporation to Backward Classes, and other Communities During 1991-92 to 2005-06

	Scheduled Caste					Scheduled Tribes				
Years	Term Loans	Working Capital Loans	Special Loans	Bridge Loans	Year-wise Total	Term Loans	Working Capital Loans	Special Loans	Bridge Loans	Year-wise Total
1991-92	140477	12616	315	0	153408	1250711	47612	3090	0	1301413
1992-93	101403	8896	400	0	110699	1114082	39523	1106	0	1154711
1993-94	58331	3664	0	0	61995	705595	14867	150	0	720612
1994-95	39319	1328	118	0	40765	798731	8595	709	2000	810035
1995-96	49999	950	0	0	50949	1096783	6123	0	0	1102906
1996-97	64711	777	0	0	65488	1036499	2384	0	0	1038883
1997-98	87932	173	0	0	88105	1214210	7342	0	0	1221552
1998-99	122313	367	0	0	122680	1470528	3639	0	0	1474167
1999-00	159284	161	0	0	159445	2427919	249	0	0	2428168
2001-01	181032	0	0	0	181032	2565475	3750	0	0	2569225
2001-02	140337	0	0	0	140337	2904319	3750	0	0	2908069
2002-03	1890300	0	0	0	1890300	2784696	2830	0	0	2787526
2003-04	162463	0	0	0	162463	2643426	939	0	0	2644365
2004-05	157837	1576	0	0	159413	3307993	2208	0	0	3310201
2005-06	222927	18226	888	0	242041	3968833	897	13583	947	3984260
Total	**3578665 (98.61)**	**48734 (1.34)**	**1721 (0.05)**	**0 (0.00)**	**3629120 (100.00)**	**29289800 (99.44)**	**144708 (0.49)**	**18638 (0.06)**	**2947 (0.01)**	**29456093 (100.00)**

Source: APSFC Annual Reports.
The figures in parentheses indicates percentages to total.

category of loans. It is distressing to note that the working capital loans, special loans, bridge loans have obtained very fewer amounts, in the total amounts assisted.

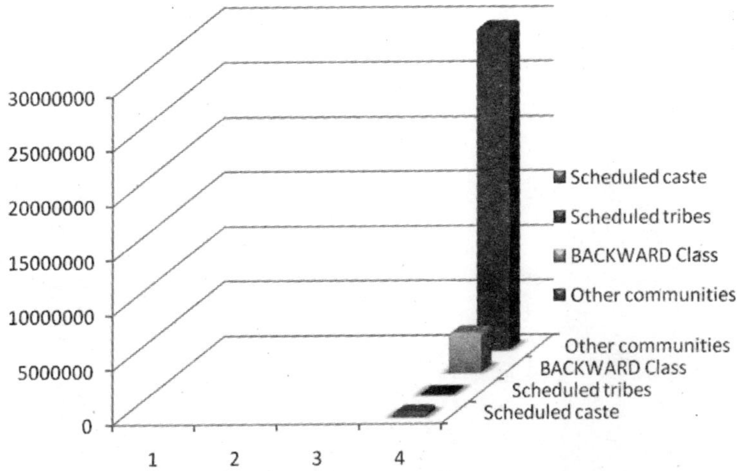

Diagram 7.1 : Disbursements Made by the Corporation to SCS STS BCS OC

Assistance made by the Corporation to Minorities

Along with weaker sections, BCs, and OCs, it is also proposed to study the assistance extended to minority communities by the Corporation. According to 2001 Census, the communities like Muslims consisting of 9.17 per cent, Christians comprising 1.55 per cent, Sikhs covering 0.04 per cent, Buddhists 0.04 per cent, Jains 0.05 per cent in the total population of the State come under the minority category.

Table 6.11 presents the number of sanctions made by the Corporation during 1991-92 to 2005-06. It is clear from the table that out of total number of 1171 sanctions, the Muslim Community received large number of sanctions (91.45%), followed by Sikhs (4.8%) and Christians (3.7%). The other minorities such as Zoroastrians and Buddhists did not obtain any sanctions. The table also shows that out of the total number of 1033 effective disbursements assisted by the

Table 6.11 : Number of Sanctions and Disbursements Extended by the Corporation to Minorities During 1991-92 to 2005-06

	Number of Effective Sanctions						Number of Effective Disbursements					
Years	Sikhs	Muslims	Christians	Zoroastrians	Neo Buddhists	Total	Sikhs	Muslims	Christians	Zoroastrians	Neo Buddhists	Total
1991-92	3	392	5	0	0	400	2	360	15	0	0	377
1992-93	3	183	20	0	0	206	6	151	9	0	0	166
1993-94	5	68	9	0	0	82	4	75	2	0	0	81
1994-95	1	50	1	0	0	52	2	39	0	0	0	41
1995-96	0	69	1	0	0	70	52	1	0	0	0	53
1996-97	3	43	2	0	0	48	1	42	2	0	0	45
1997-98	0	36	1	0	0	37	2	26	0	0	0	28
1998-99	0	41	0	0	0	41	0	35	1	0	0	36
1999-00	0	73	1	0	0	74	0	57	1	0	0	58
2000-01	NA	NA	NA	NA	NA	NA	NA	NA	NA	NA	NA	0
2001-02	NA	NA	NA	NA	NA	NA	NA	NA	NA	NA	NA	0
2002-03	0	54	1	0	0	55	0	48	1	0	0	49
2003-04	42	3	0	0	0	45	32	3	0	0	0	35
2004-05	0	35	0	0	0	35	0	40	0	0	0	40
2005-06	0	24	2	0	0	26	0	22	2	0	0	24
Total	**57** (4.87)	**1071** (91.46)	**43** (3.67)	**0** 0	**0** 0	**1171** (100.00)	**101** (9.78)	**899** (87.03)	**33** (3.19)	**0** (0.00)	**0** (0.00)	**1033** (100.00)

Source: APSFC Annual Reports.
The figures in parentheses indicates percentages to total.

Corporation, the Muslim Community claimed a major share of disbursements (87.04%), followed by Sikhs (9.77%), Christians (3.19%). However, Zoroastrians and Buddhist did not claim any disbursements.

The data pertaining to amount of effective amounts sanctioned and amount of effective disbursements are furnished in Table 7.12. As can be seen from the table, the Muslims Community received a higher share of sanctions (91.86%), while the second place is occupied by Sikhs community (4.27%), followed by Christians (3.87%). Further, the table also provides the amount of disbursements made by the Corporation to Minority Communities. In the case of disbursements also, Muslims are worked out to be the largest recipients in minority community (82.01%), followed by Sikhs (15.13%) and Christians (2.85%). The Zoroastrians, Buddhists did not claim any amounts in both sanctions and disbursements.

From the above analysis, it is concluded that even though the Corporation has been assisting the Other Communities (OCs), Backward Classes (BCs), Scheduled Castes (SCs) and Scheduled Tribes (STs), the share obtained by the OCs is larger. As the SCs and STs are recognized as weaker sections, and more are living below the poverty line, it is the responsibility of the Corporation to provide financial assistance to the weaker sections. The accessibility to funds and timely availability of assistance to these voiceless people goes a long way in achieving the 'inclusive growth'. Then only the goal of 'inclusive growth' can be achieved resulting in poverty eradication, entrepreneurship development and empowerment of the weaker sections.

Major Findings of the Study

Following are the major findings of the study

1. The analysis of the assistance made by APSFC on balanced regional development revealed that Telangana region has been accounting for a majority share in the sanction of

Table 6.12 : Amount of Sanctions and Disbursements Extended by the Corporation to Minorities During 1991-92 to 2005-06

(Amount in '000)

Years	Number of Effective Sanctions						Number of Effective Disbursements					
	Sikhs	Muslims	Christians	Zoroastrians	Neo Buddhists	Total	Sikhs	Muslims	Christians	Zoroastrians	Neo Buddhists	Total
1991-92	2146	70454	1773	0	0	74373	1051	39335	2270	0	0	42656
1992-93	2730	37910	4213	0	0	44853	2393	30750	726	0	0	33869
1993-94	7248	17992	2498	0	0	27738	1331	20423	346	0	0	22100
1994-95	915	33147	725	0	0	34787	148	9063	36	0	0	9247
1995-96	0	38297	412	0	0	38709	0	23960	304	0	0	24264
1996-97	2784	25316	546	0	0	28646	566	28499	579	0	0	29644
1997-98	0	29238	5410	0	0	34648	2043	13600	57	0	0	15700
1998-99	0	52422	0	0	0	52422	0	30046	5079	0	0	35125
1999-00	0	111982	117	0	0	112099	0	61221	738	0	0	61959
2000-01	NA	NA	NA	NA	NA	-	NA	NA	NA	NA	NA	-
2001-02	NA	NA	NA	NA	NA	-	NA	NA	NA	NA	NA	-
2002-03	0	72943	1000	0	0	73943	0	86215	1000	0	0	87215
2003-04	12186	3600	0	0	0	15786	75659	3501	0	0	0	79160
2004-05	0	68238	0	0	0	68238	0	63112	0	0	0	63112
2005-06	0	40596	8650	0	0	49246	0	41108	4549	0	0	45657
Total	**28009** (4.27)	**602135** (91.86)	**25344** (3.87)	**0** (0.00)	**0** (0.00)	**655488** (100.00)	**83191** (15.13)	**450833** (82.01)	**15684** (2.85)	**0** (0.00)	**0** (0.00)	**549708** (100.00)

Source: APSFC Annual Reports.

The figures in parentheses indicates percentages to total.

term loans in all the years of the pre-reform period with the exception of 1976-77 and 1977-78. It is also interesting to note that in the overall pre-reform period, the total loans sanctioned by APSFC amounted to Rs 1395,95,83 crores. During the post- reform period also Telangana region has secured major share in all the years without any exception.

In respect of disbursements of terms loan also Telangana region accounted for the highest percentage in the total disbursements of terms loans in all the years of pre-reform period with the exception the years 1976-77. The share of Telangana region is amazingly as high as 91.29 percent. During the post- reform period also, a major share of 64.71 percent is claimed by Telangana region followed by Andhra region (20.47%) and Rayalaseema region (14.82%). Thus both in terms of sanctions as well as disbursements of term loans by APSFC, Telangana region accounted for the highest proportion of term loans followed by Coastal Andhra and Rayalaseema regions.

2. Since 1980's there was a massive expansion in the branch network of the Corporation with a view to cover backward areas of the State. However, the analysis of the backward and forward districts revealed that some of the Backward districts were not able to get even the average amount of sanctioned loan of the State. These included Karimnagar, Warangal, Nizamabad, Kurnool, Mahabubnagar, Anantapur, Chittoor, Kadapa, Khammam, Prakasam, and Srikakulam. There were only four backward districts namely Nalgonda, Medak, Mahabubnagar and Nellore, which were able to get more than the average sanctioned loan of the State.

3. The industry-wise analysis of loan assistance sanctioned by the Corporation during the pre-reform period revealed that the chemical products industry occupied the first position by claiming 24.18 per cent of the total sanctions. Chemical industry is followed by services accounting for 12.35 per cent of total sanctions.

4. The analysis of the industry-wise disbursements in the pre reform period revealed that in terms of disbursements also same ranks with slight changes were obtained by the industries. In respect of both sanctions and disbursements also Textiles, Fisheries, Electricity Generation Supply, Petroleum Products, Transport Vehicles and spare parts received very meagre amounts of disbursements during the pre-reform period.

5. In the post-reform period Food Products accounted for a highest proportion of loan assistance sanctioned covering 3258 units. However, the sanctions decreased from 38.44 per cent in 1991-92 to 4.98 percent by 2005-06. It is disheartening to note that the total number of units also registered a decreasing trend year after year. Food products is followed by Other Industries. However, in the case of disbursements in the post reform period, the Other Industries tops the list followed by Food Industry and Chemical Industry. However, Fisheries Industry, Beverage and Tobacco, Gas Manufacturing Industry, Petroleum Products, Leather Products, Wood Products Industry, Electricity Generation Supply Industries have been getting lesser amounts of sanctions during the post-reform period.

6. The constitution-wise assistance made to MSI units revealed that the proprietary concerns accounted for the highest percentage in the total number of units assisted by the APSFC throughout the pre-reform period with the exception of the two years, i.e. 1979-80 and 1980-81. It is interesting to observe that the number of Joint Hindu Family concerns is the lowest in terms of the units to be assisted by APSFC in all the years of pre-reform period. The total number of units assisted during the post- reform period is found to be highest in respect of proprietary concerns (46.72%) followed by partnership concerns (35.35%) and private limited companies (13.05%).

In the case SSI units proprietary concerns accounted for the highest proportion i.e 73.72 percent of the total number of units in respect of disbursements made by APSFC followed by Partnership Concerns (18.94%) and Private Limited Companies (6.97%) during the total pre-reform period. The proprietary concerns claimed the largest share with 68.74 per cent, followed by partnership concerns (20.74%), private limited companies (9.56%), public limited companies (0.74%), and others (0.11%) in the post-reform period.

7. The SSI sector, being identified as priority sector due to several advantages associated with it, the APSFC appears to have been giving a special thrust to the financing of small scale industries especially since 1976-77. This may be largely due to the policy reorientation of the Government for promotion of SSI sector in order to achieve the committed socio-economic goals.

   During the pre reform period out of the total sanctions, SSIs got 87.17 per cent while MSIs received 12.83 per cent. In post reform period the percentage share of SSIs declined to 66.90 per cent, while the percentage share of MSIs increased to 33.10 per cent. In the post reform period, the percentage of disbursements to SSI units accounted to 70.45 per cent, while the percentage share of MSIs is 29.55 per cent. On the other hand, in the post reform period the percentage share of SSIs declined to 67.34 per cent and MSIs claimed 32.66 per cent. From this, it may be inferred that the sanctions and disbursements though are substantial with respect to SSIs, the percentage of sanctions has declined. On the other hand, in the case of MSIs the percentage share of sanctions and disbursements are gaining momentum.

8. In order to meet the growing demand of industrial finances, the Corporation has started to engage itself in the promotion of entrepreneurship. The corporation extends purpose-wise assistance. The categories of

purpose-wise assistance are: (I) New Projects, (II) Expansion and diversification, (III) Modernization and replacement, (IV) Rehabilitation, (V) Supplementation, and (VI) power generation. The new projects accounted for 63.66 per cent in total amount sanctioned to MSI industries during the period 1989-90 to 2005-06. The expansion and diversification projects claimed the next largest share both in terms of number and the amount of sanctions consists of 34.75 per cent. This followed by supplementation assistance of 0.65 per cent. The power generation, rehabilitation, modernization and replacement claimed very little assistance during this period.

9. In the case of SSI sector, the new projects claimed a large amount of assistance sanctioned by the Corporation both in terms of number and amount sanctioned. The new projects claimed 75.88 per cent of the total sanctions covering 32041 units. The expansion and diversification projects claimed 22.31 per cent consisting of 3218 units. It is observed that the rehabilitation and modernization/ replacements are getting lesser amounts of sanctions.

   Thus, the analysis shows that the Corporation has been rising sanctions and disbursements quite impressively, and more particularly in the post-reform period compared to the pre-reform period.

10. An analysis with respect to the association between disbursements and total recoveries shows that there is a positive correlation between these two variables. The co-efficient of correlation is 0.91and is found to be statistically significant. The comparative study of the recoveries between pre-reform period and post-reform period revealed that the performance is quite impressive during post-reform period. The SFCs have been specifically set up for the purpose of helping the business concerns of small and medium units. Though the Corporation is not established as profit making organization, it still earned some profits. The Corporation earned high profits relatively during the post- reform period.

11. An attempt is made to identify the recovery factors such as principal Recovery (PRC) and Interest Amount Collected (INTC) affecting on the Disbursements by employing regression technique.

    These revealed interesting results. There are two common features: (1) the association between disbursement and PRC is positive (or direct) in both the periods. (2) The estimated linear regression equations in both the periods are statistically significant in terms of goodness of fit and (3) the impact of PRC on Disbursement is relatively declined during the two periods of the study. In contrast to the results obtained from the functional relationship between Disbursement (DISB) and Interest Amount Collected (INTC) indicates that the value of the regression coefficient is around 2.7 during both the periods (pre-reform as well as post-reform). The explanatory power of INTC is higher than that of PRC during pre-reform period. About 98 per cent of variation is explained by INTC alone during this period.

    During the combined period, (1976-77 to 2005-06) the regression coefficients are 1.35 (when DISB is regressed on PRC and 2.05 (when DISB is regressed on INTC). Thus, the estimated values of the regression coefficients are considerably higher when DISB is regressed on INTC than its counterpart, regression coefficient when DISB is regressed on PRC during the two sub-periods as well as the combined period. From the linear empirical analysis, one can conclude that the impact of INTC is considerably higher than PRC on DISB during all the periods.

    The results of log-linear as in the lines of a linear form are obtained with the exception of interpretation of regression coefficient. The coefficient of the variable measures elasticity in the log-linear form and the marginal values in the case of linear form. If one considers the t-ratios, goodness of fit and the F-ratios, the linear form performed very well than log-linear form in almost all the regression equations.

12. An attempt is also made to compute elasticities at mean values of the variables used in the analysis of linear functional form. The values of elasticities of disbursement with respective PRC is higher (1.01) in pre-reform period than its value (0.93) in post-reform period for linear form. In the case of the log-linear form, the same elasticity is less (0.92) in the pre-reform period than its value (1.92) in post-reform period. Exactly opposite trends in elasticities of Disbursements with respective INTC are observed in each case of linear and log-linear forms.

    As far as the combined period is concerned, both the elasticities of Disbursements with respect to PRC and INTC derived from the linear form are just higher than unity (1.01 and 1.25 respectively) while, both these elasticities are inelastic (0.75 and 0.85 respectively) in the case of log-linear form. In the combined period, the impact of Interest Amount Collected on Disbursement (in terms of marginal values and elasticities) are higher than the impact of Principle Recovery on Disbursements made by Andhra Pradesh State Financial Corporation.

13. An analysis of the ranking of different schemes sanctioned by the Corporation during the selected period 1990-91 to 2005-06 revealed that the general loan scheme occupied the first position and the short term finance assistance takes second position. It is also observed that the Corporation has sanctioned only a meagre amounts to schemes such as Relief Assistance to Calamities Scheme, Scheme for Physically Handicapped, Composite Loan Scheme, Bill Discounting Scheme, Ex-service Men Scheme, Self Employment Scheme, the Scheme for 100 per cent export oriented units and Rehabilitation Scheme.

    In terms of disbursements also, the general loans schemes occupied the first position and the short term finance occupied second position. This is followed by Assistance Tourism Facility. Other schemes such as the Composite Loans, Manufacturing and Renewable Scheme, Assistance for Purchase of Mobile Van, and the 100% export oriented units have been claiming less than one per cent of the total disbursements in the same period.

14. The analysis of the total assistance made by the Corporation in terms of sanctions and disbursements to different social categories revealed that the category of 'Other Communities/Caste' received a major proportion of sanctions when compared to SCs, STs and OBCs categories. Among the minorities, Muslim Community received a higher share of sanctions (91.86%), while the Sikh Community received only meager share (4.27%), followed by Christians (3.87%). In the case of disbursements also it is observed that the Muslim Community (82.01%) is the largest recipient among the Minority Communities, followed by Sikhs (15.13%), Christians (2.85%). The Zoroastrians, Buddhists could not claim any amounts in both sanctions and disbursements.

Policy Suggestions

1. The State Financial Corporations have been given special powers under Sec.29 of SFC's Act with an objective to collect the dues expeditiously. The powers could not be effectively utilized by the State Financial Corporations due to interventions by the various Courts. The promoters are obtaining injunctions / stays on one pretext or other and therefore the amounts are blocked in these court cases. Hence, there is a need to bring an amendment enforcing the borrower to pay at least 75 per cent of the disputed amount before obtaining the interim injunction on the lines of provisions under Section 17 of Securitization and Reconstruction of Financial Assets and Enforcement of Security Interest Act, 2000. This would be a great relief for all the State Financial Corporations in effectively enforcing the powers under Section 29 of SFC's Act.
2. The branch expansion is still not adequate to meet financial requirements of small and medium scale industries in the

shall be fixed out of the credit flows. Out of the priority sector advances, a majority amount of the credit presently goes to the other communities. Therefore, there is a need to allocate a sub-target out of the total credit flows for encouraging the first generation entrepreneurs belonging to the weaker sections of the society to achieve the inclusive growth.

Conclusion

The study brings out the working of the Andhra Pradesh State Financial Corporation. The Study highlights the APSFC's committed focus on ensuring balanced regional development of the State, financing of the SME's and providing several opportunities to weaker sections of the society. In short, the Corporation has been assuming a leadership role by being a part of the exciting growth phase of the nation and a strong contributor in the dimensions of our development.

INDEX